ENJOYING ENGLISH

ENJOYING ENGLISH

BOOK 1   SADLER / HAYLLAR / POWELL

M

First published 1989 by
THE MACMILLAN COMPANY OF AUSTRALIA PTY LTD
107 Moray Street, South Melbourne 3205
6 Clarke Street, Crows Nest 2065
Reprinted 1990, 1991

Associated companies and representatives
throughout the world

National Library of Australia
cataloguing in publication data

Sadler, R. K. (Rex Kevin).
  Enjoying English. Book 1.
  ISBN 0 333 50271 X.

  1. English language — Rhetoric — Juvenile literature.
  2. English language — Composition and exercises —
  Juvenile literature. I. Hayllar, T. A. S. (Thomas Albert S.).
  II. Powell, C. J. (Clifford J.). III. Title.

808'.042

Typeset in Palatino by Savage Type Pty Ltd, Brisbane
Printed in Hong Kong

CONTENTS

PREFACE

The *Enjoying English* series is a literature-based course for secondary students. It features an extensive selection of passages drawn from high-interest, contemporary novels and non-fiction books. These constitute a base for the development of comprehension skills and additional work on language and writing skills. Because of the quality of these passages, we anticipate that students will be encouraged to read more widely by seeking out these and other similar books from libraries.

The course gives considerable emphasis to poetry and drama. The wide range of poems presented offers an opportunity for students to explore and appreciate the richness of this strand of literature. Many drama extracts and complete scripts are included, as well as creative drama projects and tasks.

The creative writing sections encourage the development of writing skills by the use of writing models and stimulus photographs. Practical language work is incorporated in each unit to reinforce and develop the students' understanding of essential language concepts.

All the material in *Enjoying English* has been thoroughly tested in the classroom to ensure that it offers rich possibilities for valuable learning and enjoyment.

MYTHS, LEGENDS AND FAMOUS TALES

1

STORIES

The First Flight

Humans have always wanted to fly. The Greek myth that follows describes a tragic first flight.

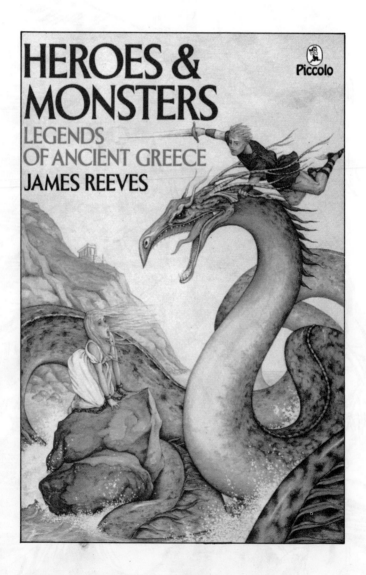

Minos kept Daedalus in Crete, making him construct marvels of ingenuity — baths and fountains, temples and statues, paved floors and splendid flights of stairs.

Then at last Daedalus grew tired of the service of King Minos and longed to return to Athens. He had brought with him to Crete his young son Icarus, and the boy too, now grown to manhood, wished to see his native land. But the craftsman could at first think of no way to escape. Crete was an island far distant from Athens, and Daedalus and his son could not build a ship in secrecy and man it for the voyage home. But his cunning brain was hard at work. At last he hit on the most daring invention of his life. Many an hour he had spent looking thoughtfully at the seabirds as they wheeled and circled about the rocky coast. 'Ah,' said he, 'if only I could fly like them! But why not? The gods have not given men wings, but they have given them a brain and hands to fashion wings for themselves.'

So in a secret place, hidden from idle curiosity, he collected together all the feathers of birds he could find, great and small. He sent his son Icarus about the island to bring back as many as he could. Then he laid them out on the ground in order — first the big feathers, then the small. When he decided he had enough, he fastened them together with wax, curving the wings like those of a bird. Icarus watched his father intently. At last the wings were finished, and Daedalus strapped them to his shoulders and went up to a piece of rising ground. Turning into the wind, he ran forward and was delighted to find himself airborne. Day after day he practised on higher and higher slopes until he reckoned the time had come to make the flight to Greece. He constructed a second pair of wings for Icarus, and together the young man and his father mastered the art of flying.

At last the day of departure came. The sun was high in the unclouded heavens, and the wind was favourable. Daedalus and Icarus carried their wings to a lofty cliff looking towards Greece and prepared for flight. When the wings were strapped firmly on their backs, Daedalus said to his son:

'Follow me. Do as I do. Don't fly too low or your wings will be weighed down with spray from the sea. Don't fly too near the sun either, or its heat will melt the wax that holds

the feathers in place. Either way you will be destroyed. Do as I say, and may the gods go with you. Now let us be off.'

So saying, he ran towards the edge of the cliff and launched himself into the air. Borne up by the wind, he journeyed straight towards his native shore.

Icarus did just as his father had done. But he was so happy to find himself aloft in the pure blue sky that he soon forgot the good advice he had been given. He wheeled and dipped like a great sea-bird, and then he soared upwards till the land and even the sea were almost out of sight. How brilliant the blazing sun appeared! Icarus was fascinated by it and could not withstand the temptation to see how high he could fly. Hotter and hotter it blazed down upon him. Too late he felt the wax on his wings begin to melt. He could not descend fast enough for the wax to cool. The wings that had borne him aloft now began to break up, and soon the ill-fated young man plunged helplessly into the sea, like a falling star. Icarus was drowned.

Daedalus had crossed the Aegean Sea and was almost home to Athens before he turned to catch sight of his son. Icarus was not to be seen. In alarm Daedalus turned and flew back to the south. It was not long before he saw, as he swooped down towards the blue waves, a pair of damaged wings floating uselessly on the sea. In sorrow Daedalus returned to Athens alone. The sea where his son had met his death was named the Icarian Sea.

from *Heroes and Monsters* by James Reeves

Reading for Understanding

1 What work did Daedalus do for King Minos?

2 Why was it difficult to escape from Crete?

3 What gave Daedalus the idea for 'the most daring invention of his life'?

4 How did Daedalus fasten the feathers together?

5 How did Daedalus prove that his invention worked?

6 What was the weather like on the day of the departure?

7 What warning did Daedalus give Icarus?

8 Why did Icarus forget his father's good advice?

9 Why did Icarus fly up towards the sun?

10 What happened when Icarus flew up towards the sun?

11 What happened to Icarus when he fell into the sea?

12 When did Daedalus realise that his son was not with him?

13 What did Daedalus then do?

14 How did Daedalus know that Icarus was dead?

15 According to the legend, why is the Icarian Sea so named?

Atalanta's Race

If Hippomenes defeats Atalanta he wins her hand in marriage. If he loses he will be executed. Now read this exciting myth to learn the outcome.

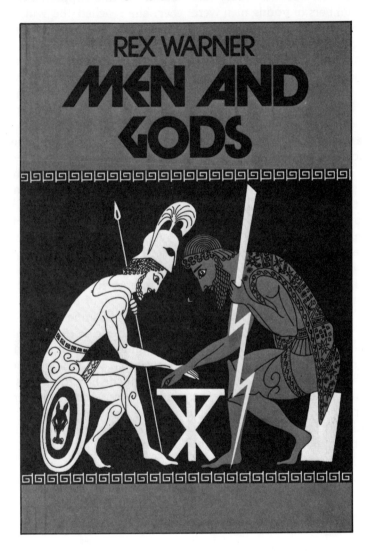

The huntress Atalanta could run faster even than the fastest runners amongst men. Nor was her beauty inferior to her swiftness of foot; both were beyond praise.

When Atalanta asked the oracle about whom she ought to marry, the god replied: 'Do not take a husband, Atalanta. If you do, it will bring disaster on you. Yet you will not escape, and though you will continue to live, you will not be yourself.'

Terrified by these words, Atalanta lived in the dark woods unmarried. There were many men who wished to marry her, but to them, in their eagerness, she said: 'No one can have me for his wife unless first he beats me in a race. If you will, you may run with me. If any of you wins, he shall have me as a prize. But those who are defeated will have death for their reward. These are the conditions for the race.'

Cruel indeed she was, but her beauty had such power that numbers of young men were impatient to race with her on these terms.

There was a young man called Hippomenes, who had come to watch the contest. At first he had said to himself: 'What man in his senses would run such a risk to get a wife?' and he had condemned the young men for being too madly in love. But when he saw her face and her body all stripped for the race — a face and a body like Venus's own — he was lost in astonishment and, stretching out his hands, he said: 'I had no right to blame the young men. I did not know the prize for which they were running.'

As he spoke, his own heart caught on fire with love for her and, in jealous fear, he hoped that none of the young men would be able to beat her in the race. Then he said to himself: 'But why should not I try my fortune? When one takes a risk, the gods help one.'

By now the race had started, and the girl sped past him on feet that seemed to have wings. Though she went fast as an arrow, he admired her beauty still more. Indeed she looked particularly beautiful when running. In the breeze her hair streamed back over her ivory shoulders; the ribbons with their bright borders fluttered at her knees; the white of her young body flushed rose-red, as when a purple awning is drawn over white marble and makes the stone glow with its own colour. While Hippomenes fixed his eyes on her, she reached the winning post and was crowned with the victor's garland. The young men, with groans, suffered the penalty of death according to the agreement which they had made.

Their fate, however, had no effect on Hippomenes. He came forward and, fixing his eyes on Atalanta, said: 'Why do you win an easy glory by conquering these slow movers? Now run with me. If I win, it will be no disgrace to you. I am a king's son and Neptune is my great grandfather. And, if you defeat me, it will be an honour to be able to say that you defeated Hippomenes.'

As he spoke, Atalanta looked at him with a softer expression in her eyes. She wondered whether she really wanted to conquer or to be conquered. She thought to herself: 'What god, envious of beautiful young men, wants to destroy this one and makes him seek marriage with me at the risk of his dear life? In my opinion, I am not worth it. It is not his beauty that touches me (though I might easily be touched by that); it is because he is still only a boy. And then there is his courage, and the fact that he is willing to risk so much for me. Why should he die, simply because he wants to live with me? I wish he would

go, while he still may, and realise that it is fatal to want to marry me. Indeed he deserves to live. If only I were happier, if only the fates had not forbidden me to marry, he would be the man that I would choose.'

Meanwhile Atalanta's father and the whole people demanded that the race should take place. Hippomenes prayed to Venus and said: 'O goddess, you put this love into my heart. Now be near me in my trial and aid me!'

A gentle breeze carried his prayer to the goddess and she was moved by it. Little time, however, remained in which she could help him. But it happened that she had just returned from her sacred island of Cyprus, where in one of her temple gardens grows a golden apple tree. The leaves are gold; the branches and the fruit rattle with metal as the wind stirs them. Venus had in her hand three golden apples which she had just picked from this tree. Now she came down to earth, making herself visible only to Hippomenes, and showed him how to use the apples.

Then the trumpets sounded and the two runners darted forward from the starting post, skimming over the sandy course with feet so light that it would seem they might have run over the sea or over the waving heads of standing corn. The crowd shouted their applause. 'Now, Hippomenes,' they cried, 'run as you have never run before! You are winning.' It would be difficult to say whether Hippomenes or Atalanta herself was most pleased with this encouragement. For some time Atalanta, though she might have passed the young man, did not do so. She ran by his side, looking into his face. Then, half unwillingly, she left him behind. He with parched throat and straining lungs followed after; still the winning post was far in the distance; and now he took one of the golden apples which Venus had given him and threw it in her way. The girl looked with wonder at the shining fruit and, longing to have it, stopped running so that she could pick it up. Hippomenes passed her and again the spectators shouted their applause. Soon, however, Atalanta made up the ground that she had lost and again left Hippomenes behind. He threw the second apple, once more took the lead and once more was overtaken. Now they were in sight of the winning post, and Hippomenes, with a prayer to Venus, threw the last apple rather sideways, so that it went some distance from the course. Atalanta seemed to hesitate whether she should go after it or not, but Venus made her go and, when she had picked up the apple, she made it heavier, handicapping the girl not only by the time she had lost but by the weight of what she was carrying. This time she could not catch Hippomenes. He passed the winning post first and claimed her as his bride.

from *Men and Gods* by Rex Warner

Reading for Meaning

1 In what ways was the huntress, Atalanta, an unusual woman?

2 Why did Atalanta live unmarried in the dark woods?

3 What did a man have to do if he wished to become Atalanta's husband?

4 What happened to him if he failed?

5 Why were there a number of young men impatient to race with Atalanta, despite the terrible penalty for defeat?

6 At first, what was Hippomenes' attitude to the young men who were going to race against Atalanta?

7 How did Hippomenes feel when he saw Atalanta's face and her body all stripped for the race?

8 Why did Atalanta look particularly beautiful when running?

9 What reasons does Hippomenes give Atalanta to convince her to race against him?

10 '. . . Atalanta looked at him with a softer expression in her eyes.' What does this reveal about Atalanta's feelings towards Hippomenes?

11 What does Atalanta mean by 'it is fatal to want to marry me'?

12 Why did Venus decide to help Hippomenes?

13 How did Venus come to have three golden apples?

14 Who was the crowd encouraging to win the race?

15 What evidence can you find to show that Hippomenes was tiring during the course of the race?

16 What did Hippomenes do with the first golden apple?

17 How did Atalanta react to the appearance of the first golden apple?

18 Why did Atalanta hesitate about going after the third golden apple?

19 What had Venus done to the third apple?

20 What did Hippomenes do after he passed the winning post?

The Sword in the Stone

This famous English legend describes how a young lad, Arthur, becomes king of England.

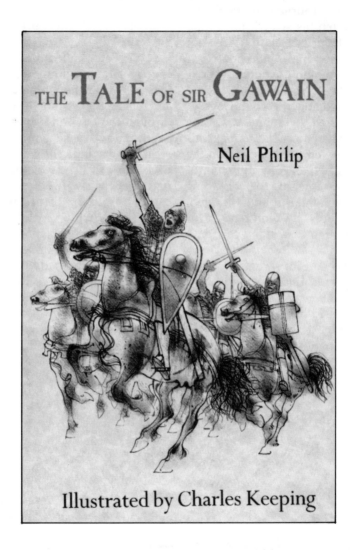

Then, one Christmas Day, Merlin reappeared, and caused a great stone to appear in a London churchyard. Set in the stone was an anvil, and sticking out of the top of the anvil was a sword. There were letters inscribed in gold upon its hilt, and they read, 'Whoso pulleth out this sword from this stone and anvil is rightwise king born of all England'.

Tongues began to wag at that. But once all the jokers had tried and failed to remove the sword, it was decided to call a tournament for New Year's Day. Every knight in the kingdom would come; surely one of them would prove to be the king. But when the day came, not one of the knights could budge the sword an inch.

When all had tried and failed to pull the

sword from the stone, the knights moved on to challenge each other on the tournament field. One of these knights was a young man from the north of England, Sir Kay. Now Sir Kay was a hasty and ill-tempered youth, and when he reached the tournament field and realised he'd forgotten his sword, his young squire, a lad about thirteen or fourteen, got the blame. Kay cuffed him, and shouted at him, and sent him running to fetch it.

But when the lad arrived at the house where they were lodging, he found everything locked and barred. Everyone was at the jousting. So he had no choice but to make his way back to Sir Kay, empty-handed. On the way back, though, he passed a churchyard, and in that churchyard he saw the very thing he wanted sticking right through the anvil into a stone: a sword. He didn't pause or think, but just took the sword and carried it to Sir Kay.

Now Sir Kay was no fool — he was never that — and he knew at once by the writing on the hilt what it was the squire had brought him. He called his father, Sir Ector, to his side, and said, 'Here is the sword from the stone. I am the rightful king of England.'

Sir Ector just looked at Kay. And then he led his son back to the churchyard, and into the church. Then he took a bible and gave it to Kay, saying, 'Son, swear to me on this holy book that you yourself removed the sword.'

'My squire, Arthur, brought it to me,' said Sir Kay.

So Sir Ector called the lad Arthur into the church, and asked him how he came by the sword. Arthur thought he was to be scolded, and seizing the weapon he ran to slide it back through the anvil into the stone. He said he hadn't meant to do wrong.

Sir Ector and Sir Kay followed Arthur back into the churchyard, and they both tugged at the sword, but it would not move. 'Arthur,' said Sir Ector, 'remove the sword again,' and Arthur withdrew it as easily as from a scabbard. Then Sir Ector and Sir Kay knelt down before him, and kissed his hand. And Arthur, who had been raised as a foster brother to Sir Kay, said, 'Father, brother, why do you kneel to me?'

Sir Ector told him, 'I am not your father, Arthur, nor is Sir Kay your brother. You are a foundling child, brought to me as a baby

by the enchanter Merlin. Since then, I have raised you as my own. I never dreamed you were King Uther's son.'

Then the lad Arthur wept, because Sir Ector was not his father, and Sir Kay was not his brother, and he was king of all England.

You can imagine the nobles and the knights were not well pleased. But not one of them could move the sword, and Arthur could do so whenever he pleased. It was the common folk — the ones who suffered most from the lawlessness of the times and the caprice of the nobles who thought everything they did was right because they did it — it was the common folk who made Arthur king.

And when he was king, it was the common folk Arthur helped most. With Kay as his steward, and Merlin as his guide, he set about restoring law and justice to the land. And to help him do so, he created the fellowship of the Knights of the Round Table, for those knights who wanted to fight wrong, and help him rule justly and wisely.

from *The Tale of Sir Gawain* by Neil Philip

Reading for Understanding

1 What did Merlin do when he reappeared?

2 What was unusual about the stone?

3 What is the meaning of the words: 'Whoso pulleth out this sword from this stone and anvil is rightwise king born of all England.'

4 What is the meaning of 'tongues began to wag'.

5 Why was it decided to call a tournament for New Year's Day?

6 What kind of person was Sir Kay?

7 Why did Sir Kay cuff and shout at his squire?

8 What did Sir Kay's squire find in a churchyard?

9 What did Sir Kay do when he was given the sword?

10 What evidence can you find to show that Sir Ector did not believe that Sir Kay had removed the sword from the stone?

11 What did Arthur do when Sir Ector asked him how he obtained the sword?

12 What happened when Sir Ector and Sir Kay tugged at the sword?

13 'I am not your father . . .' Why wasn't Sir Ector the father of Arthur?

14 Why did Arthur weep?

15 Which people did Arthur help most when he became king?

16 What did Arthur set about doing?

17 What did the Knights of the Round Table want to do?

18 What comments would you make about Arthur's character?

POETRY

The Pied Piper of Hamelin

I

Hamelin Town's in Brunswick,
By famous Hanover city;
The river Weser, deep and wide,
Washes its wall on the southern side;
A pleasanter spot you never spied;
But, when begins my ditty,
Almost five hundred years ago,
To see the townsfolk suffer so
From vermin, was a pity.

II

Rats!
They fought the dogs, and killed the cats,
And bit the babies in the cradles,
And ate the cheeses out of the vats,
And licked the soup from the cooks' own
    ladles,
Split open the kegs of salted sprats,
Made nests inside men's Sunday hats,
And even spoiled the women's chats,
By drowning their speaking
With shrieking and squeaking
In fifty different sharps and flats.

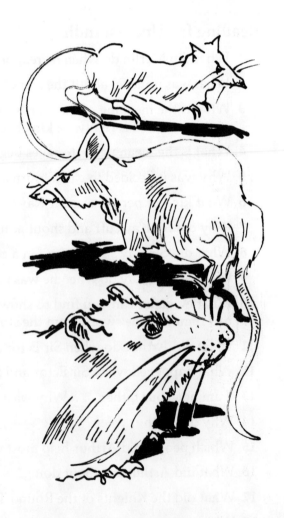

III

At last the people in a body
To the Town Hall came flocking:
' 'Tis clear,' cried they, 'our Mayor's a
    noddy;
And as for our Corporation — shocking!

To think we buy gowns lined with
　　ermine
For dolts that can't or won't determine
What's best to rid us of our vermin!
You hope, because you're old and obese,
To find in the furry civic robe ease?
Rouse up, Sirs! Give your brains a
　　racking
To find the remedy we're lacking,
Or, sure as fate, we'll send you packing!'
At this the Mayor and Corporation
Quaked with a mighty consternation.

IV

An hour they sat in council,
At length the Mayor broke silence:
'For a guilder I'd my ermine gown sell —
I wish I were a mile hence!
It's easy to bid one rack one's brain —
I'm sure my poor head aches again,
I've scratched it so, and all in vain.
Oh for a trap, a trap, a trap!'
Just as he said this, what should hap
At the chamber door, but a gentle tap?
'Bless us,' cried the Mayor, 'what's that?'
(With the Corporation as he sat,
Looking little though wondrous fat;
Nor brighter was his eye, nor moister
Than a too-long-opened oyster,
Save when at noon his paunch grew
　　mutinous
For a plate of turtle green and glutinous.)
'Only a scraping of shoes on the mat!
Anything like the sound of a rat
Makes my heart go pit-a-pat!'

V

'Come in!' — the Mayor cried, looking
　　bigger:
And in did come the strangest figure!
His queer long coat from heel to head
Was half of yellow and half of red;
And he himself was tall and thin,
With sharp blue eyes, each like a pin,
And light loose hair, yet swarthy skin,

No tuft on cheek nor beard on chin,
But lips where smiles went out and in —
There was no guessing his kith and kin!
And nobody could enough admire
The tall man and his quaint attire:
Quoth one: 'It's as my great-grandsire,
Starting up at the Trump of Doom's
　　tone,
Had walked this way from his painted
　　tombstone!'

VI

He advanced to the council-table:
And, 'Please your honours,' said he, 'I'm
　　able
By means of a secret charm to draw
All creatures living beneath the sun,
That creep or swim or fly or run,
After me so as you never saw!
And I chiefly use my charm
On creatures that do people harm,
The mole and toad and newt and viper;
And people call me the Pied Piper.'
(And here they noticed round his neck
A scarf of red and yellow stripe,
To match with his coat of the self-same
　　check;
And at the scarf's end hung a pipe;
And his fingers, they noticed, were ever
　　straying
As if impatient to be playing
Upon his pipe, as low it dangled
Over his vesture so old-fangled.)
'Yet,' said he, 'poor piper as I am,
In Tartary I freed the Cham,
Last June, from his huge swarms of
　　gnats;
I eased in Asia the Nizam
Of a monstrous brood of vampire-bats:
And as for what your brain bewilders,
If I can rid your town of rats
Will you give me a thousand guilders?'
'One? fifty thousand!' — was the
　　exclamation
Of the astonished Mayor and
　　Corporation.

VII

Into the street the Piper stept,
Smiling first a little smile,
As if he knew what magic slept
In his quiet pipe the while;
Then, like a musical adept,
To blow the pipe his lips he wrinkled,
And green and blue his sharp eyes
    twinkled
Like a candle-flame where salt is
    sprinkled;
And ere three shrill notes the pipe
    uttered,
You heard as if an army muttered;
And the grumbling grew to a mighty
    rumbling;
And out of the houses the rats came
    tumbling.
Great rats, small rats, lean rats, brawny
    rats,
Brown rats, black rats, grey rats, tawny
    rats,
Grave old plodders, gay young friskers,
Fathers, mothers, uncles, cousins,
Cocking tails and pricking whiskers,
Families by tens and dozens,
Brothers, sisters, husbands, wives —
Followed the Piper for their lives.
From street to street he piped advancing,
And step for step they followed dancing,
Until they came to the river Weser
Wherein all plunged and perished!
— Save one who, stout as Julius Caesar,
Swam across and lived to carry
(As he the manuscript he cherished)
To Rat-land home his commentary:
Which was, 'At the first shrill notes of
    the pipe,
I heard a sound as of scraping tripe,
And putting apples, wondrous ripe,
Into a cider-press's gripe:
And a moving away of pickle-tub
    boards,
And a leaving ajar of conserve-
    cupboards,
And a drawing the corks of train-oil
    flasks,

And a breaking the hoops of butter-
    casks;
And it seemed as if a voice
(Sweeter far than by harp or by psaltery
Is breathed) called out, Oh rats, rejoice!
The world is grown to one vast dry-
    saltery!
So, munch on, crunch on, take your
    nuncheon,
Breakfast, supper, dinner, luncheon!
And just as a bulky sugar-puncheon,
All ready staved, like a great sun shone
Glorious scarce an inch before me,
Just as methought it said, Come, bore
    me!
— I found the Weser rolling o'er me.'

VIII

You should have heard the Hamelin
    people
Ringing the bells till they rocked the
    steeple.
'Go,' cried the Mayor, 'and get long
    poles!
Poke out the nests and block up the
    holes!
Consult with carpenters and builders,
And leave in our town not even a trace
Of the rats!' — when suddenly, up the
    face
Of the Piper perked in the market-place,
With a 'First, if you please, my thousand
    guilders!'

IX

A thousand guilders! The Mayor looked
    blue;
So did the Corporation too.
For council dinners made rare havoc
With Claret, Moselle, Vin-de-Grave,
    Hock;
And half the money would replenish
Their cellar's biggest butt with Rhenish.
To pay this sum to a wandering fellow
With a gipsy coat of red and yellow!
'Beside,' quoth the Mayor with a
    knowing wink,
'Our business was done at the river's
    brink;
We saw with our eyes the vermin sink,
And what's dead can't come to life, I
    think.
So, friend, we're not the folks to shrink
From the duty of giving you something
    to drink,
And a matter of money to put in your
    poke;
But as for the guilders, what we spoke
Of them, as you very well know, was in
    joke.
Besides, our losses have made us thrifty.
A thousand guilders! Come, take fifty!'

X

The Piper's face fell, and he cried,
No trifling! I can't wait. Beside,
I've promised to visit by dinner time
Bagdad, and accept the prime
Of the Head-Cook's pottage, all he's rich
    in,
For having left, in the Caliph's kitchen,
Of a nest of scorpions no survivor —
With him I proved no bargain-driver,
With you, don't think I'll bate a stiver!
And folks who put me in a passion
May find me pipe to another fashion!'

XI

'How?' cried the Mayor, 'd'ye think I'll
    brook
Being worse treated than a Cook?
Insulted by a lazy ribald
With idle pipe and vesture piebald?
You threaten us, fellow? Do your worst,
Blow your pipe there till you burst?'

XII

Once more he stept into the street;
And to his lips again
Laid his long pipe of smooth straight
    cane;
And ere he blew three notes (such sweet
Soft notes as yet musician's cunning
Never gave the enraptured air)
There was a rustling, that seemed like a
    bustling
Of merry crowds justling at pitching and
    hustling,
Small feet were pattering, wooden shoes
    clattering,
Little hands clapping and little tongues
    chattering,
And, like fowls in a farm-yard when
    barley is scattering,
Out came the children running.
All the little boys and girls,
With rosy cheeks and flaxen curls,

And sparkling eyes and teeth like pearls,
Tripping and skipping, ran merrily after
The wonderful music with shouting and
    laughter.

XIII

The Mayor was dumb, and the Council
    stood
As if they were changed into blocks of
    wood,
Unable to move a step, or cry
To the children merrily skipping by —
And could only follow with the eye
That joyous crowd at the Piper's back.
But how the Mayor was on the rack,
And the wretched Council's bosoms
    beat,
As the Piper turned from the High Street
To where the Weser rolled its waters
Right in the way of their sons and
    daughters!
However he turned from South to West,
And to Koppelberg Hill his steps
    addressed,
And after him the children pressed;
Great was the joy in every breast.
'He never can cross that mighty top!
He's forced to let the piping drop,
And we shall see our children stop!'
When, lo, as they reached the mountain's
    side,
A wondrous portal opened wide,
As if a cavern was suddenly hollowed;
And the Piper advanced and the children
    followed,
And when all were in to the very last
The door in the mountain-side shut fast.
Did I say, all? No! One was lame,
And could not dance the whole of the
    way;
And in after years, if you would blame
His sadness, he was used to say, —
'It's dull in our town since my playmates
    left!
I can't forget that I'm bereft

Of all the pleasant sights they see,
Which the Piper also promised me.
For he led us, he said, to a joyous land,
Joining the town and just at hand,
Where waters gushed and fruit-trees
    grew,
And flowers put forth a fairer hue,
And everything was strange and new;
The sparrows were brighter than
    peacocks here,
And their dogs outran our fallow deer,
And honey-bees had lost their stings,
And horses were born with eagles' wings:
And just as I became assured
My lame foot would be speedily cured,
The music stopped and I stood still,
And found myself outside the Hill,
Left alone against my will,
To go now limping as before,
And never hear of that country more!'

XIV

Alas, alas for Hamelin!
There came into many a burgher's pate
A text which says, that Heaven's Gate
Opes to the Rich at as easy rate
As the needle's eye takes a camel in!
The Mayor sent East, West, North and
    South,
To offer the Piper, by word of mouth,
Wherever it was men's lot to find him,
Silver and gold to his heart's content,
If he'd only return the way he went,
And bring the children behind him.
But when they saw 'twas a lost
    endeavour,
And Piper and dancers were gone for
    ever,
They made a decree that lawyers never
Should think their records dated duly
If, after the day of the month and year,
These words did not as well appear,
'And so long after what happened here
On the Twenty-second of July,
Thirteen-hundred and seventy-six:'

And the better in memory to fix
The place of the children's last retreat,
They called it, the Pied Piper's Street —
Where anyone playing on pipe or tabor
Was sure for the future to lose his labour;
Nor suffered they hostelry or tavern
To shock with mirth a street so solemn;
But opposite the place of the cavern
They wrote the story on a column,
And on the great Church-Window
    painted
The same, to make the world acquainted
How their children were stolen away;
And there it stands to this very day.
And I must not omit to say
That in Transylvania there's a tribe
Of alien people that ascribe
The outlandish ways and dress

On which their neighbours lay such
    stress
To their fathers and mothers having risen
Out of some subterraneous prison
Into which they were trepanned
Long time ago in a mighty band
Out of Hamelin town in Brunswick land,
But how or why, they don't understand.

XV

So, Willy, let you and me be wipers
Of scores out with all men, — especially
    pipers!
And, whether they pipe us free from rats
    or from mice,
If we've promised them aught, let us keep
    our promise!

Robert Browning

Questions

1 How long ago did the events of the poem take place?

2 What problem did the townsfolk have in Hamelin?

3 Whom did the townsfolk approach to solve their problem?

4 What was unusual about the Pied Piper?

5 How does the Piper say that he can rid the town of rats?

6 What previous successes does the Piper say that he has had?

7 How do the Mayor and Corporation react to the Piper's words:
'If I can rid your town of rats
Will you give me a thousand guilders?'

8 What does the Piper do when he goes out into the street?

9 How do the rats react to the Piper's music?

10 What happened to the rats?

11 What did the Mayor and the Corporation do when the Piper asked for his thousand guilders?

12 'You threaten us, fellow? Do your worst,
Blow your pipe there till you burst!'
What did the Piper then do?

13 What do the children do when they hear the Piper's music?

14 Why didn't the Mayor and the Council stop the children from following the Piper?

15 What happened when the Piper and the children reached the side of the mountain?

16 Why was one of the children left behind?

17 According to the child left behind, what was the Piper's music like?

18 What did the Mayor do when the children had disappeared?

19 What comments would you make about the Mayor and his Corporation?

20 Do you think the Piper was justified in taking the children of Hamelin away? Why or why not?

It was Christmas time when King Arthur and his knights were feasting at Camelot castle. Suddenly the doors burst open and into the hall rode a huge knight. Everything about him was green, even his skin and hair. The huge warhorse he rode was also green, from head to hoof. The Green Knight challenged one of King Arthur's knights to strike him with an axe, and Sir Gawain accepted the challenge. The Green Knight promised to return the blow in a year's time.

from The Challenge of the Green Knight

Calmly the Green Knight knelt down
And bared his neck, tipping over his crown
His long and lovely locks. Gripping the shaft,
Gawain heaved it mightily aloft,
Then whipped it down, severing flesh and bone;
And the blade edge, spurting fire, split the stone.
The head bounced on the floor; like a ball in play,
Kicked from foot to foot it rolled away.
But the trunk, blood-spattered, neither fell nor faltered;
Though headless, yet — as if unchanged, unaltered —
It strutted along the paving stone stiff-limbed,
Picked up the head, marched to its horse and climbed
Into the saddle. Then waving its head on high,
It flashed at Guinevere each ghastly eye.

Slowly the green lips moved and spoke: 'My name
Is the Knight of the Green Chapel, my house and home
In the northern waste. This day, one year ahead,
You must search there till you find me. You took the pledge,
Before this company. Be true to it, Gawain.'

One year later.

'God go with you, Sir,' said the porter.

Away rode knight and squire over the moor,
Across the marshes, splashing through icy water
To the forest edge, where the trees were black as thunder,
A roof of dripping boughs. As they passed thereunder,
Gawain's helmet like a lantern lit the way,
The only sun that shone that dismal day.
They climbed to the open heath, where dimpling rills —
White over crag and boulder, brown in pools —
Babbled and bubbled down from the misty hills;
Upward to a wilderness of ice and snow
Where Gawain's armour seemed to blaze and glow
Like a fire that gave no warmth — for the steel was cold,
Cold as the clouds on ridge and peak unrolled.

They halted. 'Sir,' said the squire, 'we are near the place,
Haunt of the Green Knight, of rogues on earth
The first in violence and height and girth,
The most cruel, the most merciless
And quarrelsome. Approach him if you will,
But whoever passes he thinks it sport to kill.
One single blow from his club, one cutlass hack
Is enough. Oh, Sir, for Jesus's sake, turn back!
I swear I will never breathe a word you fled!'

'You seek my safety. Thank you,' Sir Gawain said.
But I must press on, for only cowards run.
God will protect his servant.'

Ian Serraillier

Little Red Riding Hood and the Wolf

As soon as Wolf began to feel
That he would like a decent meal,
He went and knocked on Grandma's door.
When Grandma opened it, she saw
The sharp white teeth, the horrid grin,
And Wolfie said, 'May I come in?'
Poor Grandmamma was terrified,
'He's going to eat me up!' she cried.

And she was absolutely right.
He ate her up in one big bite.
But Grandmamma was small and tough,
And Wolfie wailed, 'That's not enough!
'I haven't yet begun to feel
'That I have had a decent meal!'
He ran around the kitchen yelping,
'I've *got* to have a second helping!'
Then added with a frightful leer,
'I'm therefore going to wait right here
'Till Little Miss Red Riding Hood
'Comes home from walking in the wood.'
He quickly put on Grandma's clothes
(Of course he hadn't eaten those).
He dressed himself in coat and hat.
He put on shoes and after that
He even brushed and curled his hair,
Then sat himself in Grandma's chair.
In came the little girl in red.
She stopped. She stared. And then she said,
'What great big ears you have, Grandma.'
'All the better to hear you with,' the Wolf replied.
'What great big eyes you have, Grandma,'
    said Little Red Riding Hood.
'All the better to see you with,' the Wolf replied.

He sat there watching her and smiled.
He thought, I'm going to eat this child.
Compared with her old Grandmamma
She's going to taste like caviare.

Then Little Red Riding Hood said, *'But Grandma,*
what a lovely great big furry coat you have on.'

'That's wrong!' cried Wolf. 'Have you forgot
'To tell me what BIG TEETH I've got?
'Ah well, no matter what you say,
I'm going to eat you anyway.'
The small girl smiles. One eyelid flickers.
She whips a pistol from her knickers.
She aims it at the creature's head
And *bang bang bang* she shoots him dead.
A few weeks later, in the wood
I came across Miss Riding Hood.
But what a change! No cloak of red,
No silly hood upon her head.
She said, 'Hello, and do please note
'My lovely furry WOLFSKIN COAT.'

Roald Dahl

Questions

1 Why does the Wolf knock on Grandma's door?

2 Why was poor Grandma terrified?

3 Why does the Wolf want to eat Little Red Riding Hood?

4 Why does the Wolf complain when Little Red Riding Hood says, 'But Grandma, what a lovely big furry coat you have on'?

5 'The small girl smiles'. Why does Little Red Riding Hood smile?

6 'My lovely furry WOLFSKIN COAT'. What has happened?

7 What parts of Roald Dahl's poem did you enjoy? Why?

8 What similarities are there between Roald Dahl's poem and the original story of *Little Red Riding Hood*?

9 Do you think Roald Dahl's poem is better than the original story? Why or why not?

10 Which character did you like most in this poem?

Pegasus was a horse with great wings that carried him through the air like a bird. He had sprung from the severed head of Medusa.

Pegasus

From the blood of Medusa
Pegasus sprang.
His hoof of heaven
Like melody rang.
His whinny was sweeter
Than Orpheus' lyre,
The wing on his shoulder
Was brighter than fire.

His tail was a fountain
His nostrils were caves,
His mane and his forelock
Were musical waves,

He neighed like a trumpet,
He cooed like a dove,
He was stronger than terror
And swifter than love.

He could not be captured,
He could not be bought,
His rhythm was running,
His standing was thought.
With one eye on sorrow
And one eye on mirth
He galloped in heaven
And gambolled on earth.

And only the poet
With wings to his brain
Can mount him and ride him
Without any rein,
The stallion of heaven
The steed of the skies,
The horse of the singer
Who sings as he flies.

Eleanor Farjeon

WRITING

DESCRIBING PEOPLE

Here is a description of Mr Twit from Roald Dahl's book *The Twits*. What do you especially notice about Mr Twit? How has Roald Dahl created this impression?

MR TWIT

Mr Twit was one of these very hairy-faced men. The whole of his face except for his forehead, his eyes and his nose, was covered with thick hair. The stuff even sprouted in revolting tufts out of his nostrils and ear-holes.

Mr Twit felt that his hairiness made him look terrifically wise and grand. But in truth he was neither of these things. Mr Twit was a twit. He was born a twit. And now at the age of sixty, he was a bigger twit than ever.

The hair on Mr Twit's face didn't grow smooth and matted as it does on most hairy-faced men. It grew in spikes that stuck out straight like the bristles of a nailbrush.

And how often did Mr Twit wash this bristly nailbrushy face of his?

The answer is NEVER, not even on Sundays.

He hadn't washed it for years.

from *The Twits* by Roald Dahl

Here is another description. This one is of Mrs Dubose. What impression does the writer give of this woman?

MRS DUBOSE

She was horrible. Her face was the colour of a dirty pillowcase, and the corners of her mouth glistened with wet, which inched like a glacier down the deep grooves enclosing her chin. Old-age liver spots dotted her cheeks, and her pale eyes had black pinpoint pupils. Her hands were knobby, and the cuticles were grown up over her fingernails. Her bottom plate was not in, and her upper lip protruded; from time to time she would draw her nether lip to her upper plate and carry her chin with it. This made the wet move faster.

from *To Kill a Mockingbird* by Harper Lee

The final description is of Dallas Winston, a hood. What are some of the things that you notice about Dally?

DALLY

If I had to pick the real character of the gang, it would be Dallas Winston—Dally. I used to like to draw his picture when he was in a dangerous mood, for then I could get his personality down in a few lines. He had an elfish face, with high cheekbones and a pointed chin, small, sharp animal teeth, and ears like a lynx. His hair was almost white it was so blond, and he didn't like haircuts, or hair oil either, so it fell over his forehead in wisps and kicked out in the back in tufts and curled behind his ears and along the nape of his neck. His eyes were blue, blazing ice, cold with a hatred of the whole world. Dally had spent three years on the wild side of New York and had been arrested at the age of ten. He was tougher than the rest of us—tougher, colder, meaner.

from *The Outsiders* by S. E. Hinton

WRITING YOUR OWN DESCRIPTIONS

In a paragraph for each, write a physical description of three of the following people. Try to describe some of these features: hair, nose, eyes, eyebrows, mouth, lips, head, forehead, skin, mannerisms, hands, arms, legs, height, voice, walk, gestures and clothes.

- teacher
- headmaster
- sister
- brother
- mother
- father

- uncle
- aunt
- nephew
- niece
- friend
- enemy

- grandmother
- grandfather
- dentist
- doctor
- neighbour
- politician

- newsagent
- sportsperson
- filmstar
- television personality
- farmer
- bus driver

SPORTS PERSON   TV PERSONALITY

LANGUAGE

NOUNS

A noun is a naming word. It is a word used to name:

- people: boy, girl, Paul Hogan, Steffi Graf
- places: hospital, cinema, Paris, Russia
- things: rain, sun, moon, September, pencil, Volkswagen
- qualities: love, hate, generosity, stupidity

Now look at how Kenneth Grahame, in the first paragraph of *The Wind in the Willows*, has used nouns to create a vivid picture of the Mole doing his spring-cleaning. All the words in heavy type are nouns.

MOLE'S SPRING-CLEANING

The **Mole** had been working very hard all the **morning**, spring-cleaning his little **home**. First with **brooms**, then with **dusters**; then on **ladders** and **steps** and **chairs**, with a **brush** and a **pail** of **whitewash**; till he had **dust** in his **throat** and **eyes**, and **splashes** of **white-wash** all over his black **fur**, and an aching **back** and weary **arms**.

from *The Wind in the Willows* by Kenneth Grahame

People and Places

Match up the people in the left-hand column with the appropriate places in the right-hand column.

People	Places
king	laboratory
teacher	surgery
astronomer	barracks
artist	nursery
doctor	casino
scientist	palace
gambler	embassy
babies	stage
barrister	observatory
soldier	studio
ambassador	court
actor	school

Who Am I?

Identify the correct noun in the box for each of the following people.

cannibal	umpire	pilot	genius
pirate	orphan	removalist	invalid
assassin	pianist	shepherd	pedestrian
burglar	spectator	author	witch

1 I steal from houses and shops.

2 I am too ill to do things for myself.

3 I am a hired murderer.

4 I am exceptionally intelligent.

5 I eat human flesh.

6 I am a sea robber.

7 I travel about on foot.

8 I am a woman supposed to possess magical powers.

9 I act as a judge in a game.

10 My parents are dead.

11 I am one who watches a sporting event.

12 I play the piano.

13 I move furniture.

14 I look after sheep.

15 I write books.

16 I fly a plane.

What Place Is This?

For each definition, write down a noun from the box.

quarry	garage	stable	prison
silo	laundry	hangar	wharf
hive	kennel	bakery	reservoir
gymnasium	aquarium	factory	library

1 Books are kept here.

2 Stone is mined here.

3 Horses are housed here.

4 This is where large ships tie up.

5 This is where criminals stay.

6 Water is stored here.

7 This is where planes are kept.

8 This is where grain is stored.

9 Bees live here.

10 Bread is made here.

11 This is where some people exercise.

12 Goods are made here.

13 Cars are repaired here.

14 This is where washing is done.

15 Dogs often live in one of these.

16 A place where pet fish are kept.

Opposites

Write down next to each noun, another noun opposite in meaning. The first letter has been given to help you.

1 danger   s...................

2 love   h...................

3 war   p...................

4 poverty   w...................

5 dwarf   g...................

6 defeat   v...................

7 failure   s...................

8 punishment   r...................

9 coward   h...................

10 ignorance   k...................

11 captivity   f...................

12 questions   a...................

13 arrival   d...................

14 enemy   f...................

15 entrance   e...................

16 depth   h...................

17 loss   g...................

18 master   s...................

19 age   y...................

20 cruelty   k...................

Meanings

Explain how the nouns in each group differ in meaning.

1 lady lass female
2 diary atlas novel
3 lane highway street
4 handbag briefcase suitcase
5 canoe launch submarine
6 lounge bench throne
7 city suburb port
8 burglar kidnapper murderer
9 nightmare dream hibernation
10 portrait cartoon sketch
11 picnic barbecue snack
12 mansion shack cottage

PUNCTUATION

CAPITAL LETTERS AND FULL STOPS

We write in sentences so that our words will be easier to read and understand. A sentence begins with a capital letter and ends with a full stop.

Example: <u>A</u>t last the day of departure came<u>.</u>

Correctly punctuate with capital letters and full stops these sentences from 'The First Flight'.

1 icarus did just as his father had done
2 too late he felt the wax on his wings begin to melt
3 hotter and hotter it blazed down upon him
4 he could not descend fast enough for the wax to cool
5 icarus was not to be seen
6 the sea where his son had met his death was named the Icarian Sea
7 icarus was drowned
8 but the craftsman could at first think of no way of escape
9 the sun was high in the unclouded heavens, and the wind was favourable
10 borne up by the wind, he journeyed straight to his native shore

DRAMA

Odious Underarmus, Marathon Man

Bill Condon and Dianne Bates

This one-act play presents a humorous version of the origin of the Olympic Games.

CHARACTERS

Odious Underarmus fishmonger
Billious Odious's friend
Jilly Achilles a maiden
Regurgitus Jilly's handmaiden
Achilles Jilly's father
Tyrannus Dreadus Jilly's betrothed
Narratus
The Oracle
A crowd

SCENE 1

A crowded market place in ancient Greece.

Odious (*Calling*) Salmon, snapper, sardines, stingray, shark, squid, shrimps, swordfish, sole, sturgeon, seal! Freshly caught last week! Getcha red-hot fishies. Salmon, snapper . . .

> (*He continues to mime as Narratus steps forward from the crowd.*)

Narratus Ladies and gentlemen, welcome to a typical day in the tiny Grecian village of Athos in the year 776 BC. Behind me is a typical smelly fishmonger of these parts, Odious Underarmus, selling typically smelly fish. What Odious does not realise is that at any minute the course of his life is going to dramatically change — in fact, what you are about to witness is the beginning of a 'wimpsical' romance.

> (*Jilly, Achilles and Regurgitus enter.*)

Regurgitus   Hurry along now, Jilly. You know we'll be in trouble if they find out we're from Sparta.

Jilly   Don't be so cowardly, Regurgitus; a Spartan has no fear of anything, let alone these imbecilic Athenians.

Odious   Salmon, snapper, sea lion, stingray. Getcha red-hot fishies. Fish, miss? Care for some week-old fishies?

Jilly   Do you have any smoked shicklebocks?

Odious   I smoked the last one yesterday, miss.

Jilly   Well, do you have any nice eyes?   (*Pause*)   Why did I say nice eyes?

Odious   Because you have — you have got nice eyes.

Regurgitus   Oh, oh! I've seen that look before.

Narratus   The look of love!

Regurgitus   Exactly! I don't like the look of this. Hurry, Jilly! Let's go.

Jilly   (*To Odious*)   I do like your looks, Mr . . . Mr . . . ?

Odious   Odious Underarmus, miss.

Regurgitus   This can't go any further, Jilly. Your father would never agree to you having anything to do with an Athenian.

Jilly   An oracle once told me I would hook the man of my dreams . . .

Odious   My mum always said I was a good catch.

Regurgitus   But Jilly, he's got a flat head!

Jilly   'Jilly Achilles,' the oracle said,
'You'll swim in the waters of love,
A fishmonger you'll wed!'

Regurgitus   But you can't marry this Odious Underarmus; you're betrothed to Tyrannus Dreadus.

(Billious enters.)

Billious   Did someone say 'Tyrannus Dreadus'? I just saw him! He's heading this way, and boy, is he angry!

Narratus   Tyrannus Dreadus, hero of Sparta, Mr Mediterranean Muscles titleholder for the last five years, champion lion wrestler and champion chariot thrower, undisputed best and unfairest champ in all sports in the known world.

Billious   He's looking for his betrothed, Jilly Achilles.

Odious   Billious, my best friend, allow to introduce my fiance . . .

Billious   Really? Wow! How did a wimp like you get such a beautiful maiden, Odious?

Jilly   It was love at first sight.   *(She shakes hands vigorously with Billious)*   How do you do, Billious? I'm Jilly Achilles.

Billious   Jilly Achilles?! Odious, you're mincemeat when Tyrannus finds you.

Odious   I'm infatuated, hopelessly in love. She's the most beautiful maiden I ever set eyes on. Nothing can ever stop me from loving her.

Billious   But Tyrannus kills 100 slaves a day — just for practice!

Odious   It's off. Sorry, Jilly. The engagement's over. I hear my mother calling.

Regurgitus   Oh good! Come on, Jilly. Let's go!

Jilly   Fiddle dee dee! I'm going to get my man. Follow me, Odious. Daddy will sort this out for us.

Billious   But it's well known that your father hates Spartans.

Odious   Who's your father?

Jilly   My mother's husband. The great warrior Achilles. But don't worry about Daddy. I know his weakness.

(Exit Jilly dragging Odious, with Regurgitus in pursuit.)

SCENE 2

Achilles' home. Achilles is rubbing his heel. Enter Jilly.

Jilly   Daddy!

Achilles   My dearest daughter!

Jilly   Are you still having trouble with your heel?

Achilles   Yes, my sandals are killing me.

Jilly   I've got just the thing to fix that. Here you are, a gift.

(She gives him a pair of thongs.)

Achilles   What are they, Jilly?

Jilly   Thongs. Try them.

(Achilles puts them on.)

Achilles   Nice! Wonderful! My favourite daughter, you've saved me so much pain!

Jilly   I'd do anything for you, Daddy.

Achilles   I'd do anything for you, my daughter.

Jilly   Really? Anything?

Achilles   Just name it.

Jilly   (*Calling*)   You can come in now, my sweetheart!

(*Odious enters.*)

Jilly   Daddy, this is the man of my dreams.
Achilles   The man of your dreams? Jilly dear, he's odious!
Jilly   Daddy, how did you know?
Achilles   I could smell him, of course! This man is off! Get him out of here!
Jilly   But I'm going to marry him.
Odious   And I'm going to marry her — if that's all right.
Achilles   No, it's not all right. She's betrothed to Tyrannus Dreadus.
Jilly   Daddy, you said you'd do anything for me, right?
Achilles   Oh, all right.
Jilly   Then banish Tyrannus to the Dead Sea. And give your blessing for Odious to marry me — even if he is an Athenian.
Achilles   Athenian! Spartans hate Athenians!
Jilly   Daddy, you promised.
Achilles   Oh, this makes it difficult. If it were found out I gave my permission so easily — if only the Oracle were here to advise me.

(*The Oracle enters, running.*)

Oracle   You rang?
Achilles   Oh, Oracle, what should I do? Here's the story: I had this bad heel see, and my daughter . . .
Oracle   Enough! The Oracle knows all. Here is the answer to your dilemma . . .   (*Pauses*)   But first, dilemmas don't come cheap, Achilles.
Achilles   How much?
Oracle   Fifty drachmas.
Achilles   Do you take Greekcard?
Oracle   Of course. And American Express.
Odious   Yes, American Express is good. I never leave Rome without it.
Oracle   Quiet! I'm the Oracle. I'll tell the jokes. Right, here's the answer to your dilemma, Achilles:

(*He goes into a trance.*)

If Odious and Jilly be wed,
Tyrannus Dreadus must be dead.
Achilles   Aha! An evil plot!
Oracle   Be quiet, you fool . . .
The answer is thus —
Odious wins at Mount Olympus.
Jilly   (*To Odious*)   What do you think, my darling?
Odious   He's a dreadful poet.
Achilles   Yes! Yes! I've just had this brilliant idea! I'll invent something called the Olympic Games — held at Mount Olympus . . . a friendly contest to the death between Spartans and Athenians. And Jilly, if your Athenian beats Tyrannus Dreadus, you two can go off and get hitched.

SCENE 3

On Mount Olympus. Odious and Tyrannus (and others) are on their starting blocks surrounded by a crowd of people, including Jilly, Regurgitus, Billious, Achilles and Narratus.

Narratus   Warriors and maidens, welcome to the inaugural Olympic Games, proudly brought to you by our sponsors, Olympic Tyres, manufacturers of steelcat chariot wheels — when only the best will do . . .

Regurgitus   Oh, get on with it!

Narratus   The tension is enormous here today as the contestants prepare to meet the challenge of what will be known in future as the Ouzo Race.

Achilles   Pardon me. As Managing Director of Olympic Tyres, I'd like to name the contest after my home town, Marathon.

Narratus   Oh very well — the Marathon Race will take place over five days, during which time we expect many of the contestants to drop dead from fatigue, not to mention sore feet . . .

(He mimes more speech-making as attention focuses on Tyrannus and Odious.)

Tyrannus   You're going to die, Odious.

Odious   But death is so permanent. And I have to come back to marry my Jilly.

Tyrannus   That did it! You've made me angry! Now you'll *really* suffer! When this race starts, I'll catch you and tear you apart.

Odious   But that could be painful!

Jilly   You're going to have to outrun him, Odious!

Tyrannus   Ha, ha! No one can outrun me! And when I get you, Athenian, I'll run my sword through you . . .

Odious   *(Hysterically)* Oh, pain!

Tyrannus   . . . I'll gouge out your eyes . . .

Odious Agony!
Tyrannus . . . and then I'll carry your head back on my shield to Jilly!
Odious Bandaids!
Jilly Odious?
Odious What?
Jilly Remember, whatever you do, keep your head!
Narratus On your marks, get set — go!

(The contestants begin, Odious sprinting ahead of the field as Tyrannus charges after him with his sword.)

SCENE 4

Mount Olympus. A crowd has gathered, including Jilly, Regurgitus, Narratus, Billious and Achilles.

Narratus And here we are at the finishing line after five days of gruelling competition in the Marathon. The winner is expected to cross the line at any moment.
Jilly And here they come!

(All peer into the distance.)

Regurgitus Jumping Grecian gods! You're right! I can't see anything, but that smell, it's the fishmonger!
Jilly And he's winning.
Achilles Yes, I see them now. Tyrannus is just behind him, brandishing his sword.

(Odious and Tyrannus enter. Odious is just in front. Both are exhausted.)

Narratus They're neck and neck, nose and nose. Photo! Odious's big nose has crossed the line first.

(Odious collapses, panting. The crowd gathers around him, ignoring Tyrannus. Achilles places a crown of laurel leaves on Odious's head.)

Tyrannus Jilly! Jilly! I fear I am about to die. I beg you, hold my hand as I pass from this world.
Jilly Oh excuse me, Odious. I'll be straight back as soon as he's snuffed it. *(She holds Tyrannus's hand.)*
Tyrannus Fairest maiden, I know you never truly loved me. But I want you to know I'm happy to die in the quest for your hand and for your heart. I will love you eternally.
Jilly Oh Tyrannus, that's the most romantic thing anyone ever said to me.
Tyrannus Oh really? Well, wait till you hear this. I love you more than . . . *(He takes an enormous breath of air and dies)*
Jilly Tyrannus, my one true love! Come back!
Achilles *(Pushing Odious towards Jilly)* He's all yours now, my daughter.
Odious Unaccustomed as I am to public speaking . . .
Jilly Oh shut up!

Regurgitus   But Jilly, that's no way to speak to your future husband.

Jilly   Ha! Did he give his life for me? No! All he did was win a silly race.

Achilles   What are you saying, Jilly?

Jilly   After careful consideration I've decided Regurgitus was right — he *has* got a flat head! Tyrannus was the only man for me. And now he's gone!

Achilles   What will you do?

Jilly   I shall spend the rest of my days living in a cave. And by the way, Odious, you're odious!

(Jilly, Regurgitus, Narratus and Achilles exit.)

Odious   I can't believe it! This is the worst day of my life . . .

Billious   Never mind, Odious. Look on the bright side.

Odious   What bright side?

Billious   (*Looking around*)   We've got a crowd here. And I've got some fish.

(They exchange knowing looks, then simultaneously yell.)

Salmon, snapper, sardines, stingray. . .

Questions

1 Where does the action of this play take place?

2 What did Odious Underarmus do for a living?

3 What are Odious's feelings towards Jilly Achilles?

4 What kind of a person is Tyrannus Dreadus?

5 Why is Achilles pleased about Jilly's present to him?

6 Why doesn't Achilles like Odious?

7 What happened to Tyrannus at the end of the Marathon race?

8 What are Jilly's feelings toward Odious at the end of the play?

9 How would you dress if you were playing the part of (a) Odious Underarmus, (b) Jilly Achilles, (c) Tyrannus Dreadus?

10 Which character in the play did you like most? Why?

11 Which section of the play did you like best? Why?

12 What problems do you think there would be in staging this play?

THE
GREEN
YEARS

2

NOVELS

Harvey

One summer, Carlie, Harvey and Thomas J. went to a foster home to live. Betsy Byars tells their moving story in her novel *The Pinballs*.

One summer two boys and a girl went to a foster home to live together.

One of the boys was Harvey. He had two broken legs. He got them when he was run over by his father's new Grand Am.

The day of his accident was supposed to be one of the happiest of Harvey's life. He had written an essay on 'Why I Am Proud to Be an American', and he had won third prize. Two dollars. His father had promised to drive him to the meeting and watch him get the award. The winners and their parents were going to have their pictures taken for the newspaper.

When the time came to go, Harvey's father said, 'What are you doing in the car?' Harvey had been sitting there, waiting, for fifteen minutes. He was wearing a tie for the first time in his life. 'Get out, Harvey, I'm late as it is.'

'Get out?'

'Yes, get out.'

Harvey did not move. He sat staring straight ahead. He said, 'But this is the night I get my award. You promised you'd take me.'

'I didn't *promise*. I said I would if I could.'

'No, you promised. You said if I'd quit bugging you about it, you'd take me. You promised.' He still did not look at his father.

'Get out, Harvey.'

'No.'

'I'm telling you for the last time, Harvey. Get out.'

'Drive me to the meeting and I'll get out.'

'You'll get out when I say!' Harvey's father wanted to get to a poker game at the Elks Club, and he was already late. 'And I say you get out *now*.' With that, the father leaned over, opened the door and pushed Harvey out of the car.

Harvey landed on his knees in the grass. He jumped to his feet. He grabbed for the car door. His father locked it.

Now Harvey looked at his father. His father's face was as red as if it had been turned inside out.

Quickly Harvey ran round the front of the car to try to open the other door. When he was directly in front of the car, his father accidentally threw the car into drive instead of reverse. In that wrong gear, he pressed the accelerator, ran over Harvey and broke both his legs.

The court had taken Harvey away from his father and put him in the foster home 'until such time as the father can control his drinking and make a safe home for the boy'.

from *The Pinballs* by Betsy Byars

Reading for Meaning

1 How did Harvey come to have two broken legs?

2 Why should the day of Harvey's accident have been the happiest of his life?

3 'He was wearing a tie for the first time in his life.' Why do you think Harvey was wearing a tie?

4 'Yes, get out.' Why didn't Harvey want to get out of the car?

5 On what condition does Harvey say he is prepared to get out of the car?

6 Where did Harvey's father want to be?

7 Why was Harvey's father in such a hurry?

8 How did Harvey's father get Harvey out of the car?

9 Why couldn't Harvey get back into the car?

10 Why did Harvey run around the front of the car?

11 In what way was it an accident when Harvey was run over?

12 How long did Harvey have to remain in the foster home?

13 What did you learn about the character of Harvey's father from your reading of this passage?

14 What are your feelings towards Harvey?

15 Do you think the court did the right thing by putting Harvey in a home? Explain your viewpoint.

Gowie Corby in Trouble

Despite all his cunning, Gowie Corby is unable to avoid what's coming to him from the team.

On Friday when I breeze in, fairly cheery, 'cos it's nearly Saturday, I find a note waiting for me. It says:

'LOOK OUT CORBY YOUR GOING TOO GET WOTS COMING TO YOU.'

Then when we come out of Assembly there's another.

'DEATH TO YOU SCUM.'

I don't find that nice at all, and spend most of the morning watching them all, wondering who sent it. The last one of the day reads:

'WE'VE GOT A GANG ONTO YOU ROTTEN SWINE AND WERE GOING TO DUFF YOU UP SO YOU WISH YOUD NEVER BEEN BORN, SO LOOK OUT YOU BEAST.'

Pathetic.

Some time later, near hometime, I don't find it so pathetic. At the end of a long, draggy, boring Friday afternoon, it's at last time to clear up. Soon, very soon, the classroom empties, only Heather and a coupla girls left, and Darren, who's reading and has forgotten he's supposed to be going home.

'Where is everybody? They disappear fast,' I say.

The girls' faces go tight and closed up. I know that look. It means that someone is being kept out of the know, and it's often been me in the past, and it's me now.

'Somethin' goin' on,' I say to them.

The girls move away, but I stop Heather near the door, seize her right ear and twist it. She squeals. The other two depart as if there are bombs in the classroom.

'Now talk. What's goin' on?'

'Nuthin'.' She whimpers as I twist a little harder and drag her to the cloakroom, to keep out of Merchant's way.

'Talk.'

'They're gonna duff you in.'

'Where?'

'Outside school. . .'

'Who?'

'They'll hurt me if I tell you. . .'

'I'll hurt you worse. You're just born unlucky. Talk.'

'Ow. Please. Don't.'

'I'll stop if you tell me who's in it.'

'The team, mostly.'

'Why?'

'They're fed up with you 'cos you're so horrible. Oh, stop, stop. I'll tell Sir.'

'No, you won't.'

'Let me go. Please, oh, please.'

'Where are they now?'

'You usually go to the shop on the corner after school, for some chewing gum.'

'Who told you?'

'Everybody knows.'

'Go on. . .'

'They're waiting for you in the alley way at the back of the shop. That's all I know, honest. Let me go, now.'

'Get out.' I push her through the door. She makes me feel sick. I feel sick anyway. Some of the kids in the team are a horrible size. Stewpid is bigger than Mr Merchant. Not that he'll be doin' much with *his* elbow.

I walk slowly into the playground. Most of the kids have gone home by now. What am I to do? Fancy that lot ganging up on me. I must go very carefully. Think . . . think. I'd better go another way home, the long way round.

And Miss Plum walks through the playground carrying two heavy bags, and in a flash I am beside her, smiling a face full of teeth like Tom in a Tom and Jerry cartoon.

'Miss Plum, please let me carry your bags. You look so laden.'

She looks surprised as well. My nice smile is almost splitting my face. She hands over the bags and we walk along side by side. I start to talk to her.

'I expect that you are looking forward to the weekend, Miss Plum. It must be a relief to get away from an awful mob like us.'

'Oh, you're not that bad, really. But you are right in a way. I do enjoy the weekends.'

'Have you a hobby, Miss? I like to go bird watching when I get the time.'

'Do you indeed, Gowie? Now, that's very interesting.'

On we walk, discussing hobbies, like two old geezers, and she tells me how nice it is to talk to me like this, as sometimes she feels she hasn't got to know me as well as she would have liked. The corner shop comes into view, with JJ's ugly mug peering round it, and jerking back at the sight of me, and I am killing myself with laughter inside as Miss Plum and I walk right past, together. I bet they're mad. I bet they're astonished. I smile at Miss Plum with all my available teeth. She does a cherry. We go right past and down the road and I'm safe. I've mucked up their dirty little plan. Load of morons. On we go, well away from the scene of danger.

'I catch a bus here,' she says. 'Thank you for your company, Gowie.'

She smiles at me as if she really likes me. I could fancy her if she wasn't so old and a teacher.

''Ave a good weekend, Miss.'

I run on till I come to the cul-de-sac where I live, Nelson Place, for heroes to live in, my grandad used to say. There are only three terrace houses, and a warehouse and some trees opposite. My house is the last one. The house next door has been empty for ages, ever since old man Pearson went bananas in the middle of the night, and chased his old woman outside in her nightgown. Round and round a car they ran in the moonlight with him waving a knife at her. I was watching out of the bedroom window and in the end the police arrived and took old Pearson away, then she left and since then the house has been empty.

I run along, happy with the Friday freedom feel, all the weekend stretching ahead, just for me, nobody saying do this, do that, go here, go there, Gowie Corby. And it's even better because I've outwitted the TEAM, and there should be something good on telly tonight, and I wonder what there is to eat. I get out my key and open the door, and suddenly, crash, stab, bam, bang, I am hit from behind, all hell breaks loose, and pain swells from nowhere to everywhere till I want to scream, and I go down on my knees, I'm jumped, ambushed, boys everywhere, hitting, kicking, I try to cover my head, my body. The pavement's hard, it tears my trousers, gashes my knees, scrunch, scrape, blood, warm and wet. Blood and salt in my mouth, tears pouring, singing in my ears, I can't see, I'm hurt, I'm scared, I can't think, I can't fight, there are too many of them, help me, help me somebody, help me please, why won't somebody come, help, no one will, no one ever did, no one, there's only you and all of them . . . lie still . . . play dead . . . lie still . . . lie dead . . . perhaps I am dead . . . voices above the grunts . . .

'That's for Stewart's elbow . . .' I feel sick.

'Are you sorry, Corby?' Oh, stop, leave me.

'Say you're sorry, Corby.' I feel sick. Leave me alone . . . alone . . .

Stewart's voice. Gruff. Anxious? Far away?

'Pack it in. We've gone too far . . . come on . . .'

It's dark. I hurt. Help, help me . . .

Another noise, a different voice. A door opening? A voice like those on the telly, cutting through the noise.

'What are you doing? Are you mad? Leave him alone!'

And everywhere is filled with the sound of running feet, running away. Someone drops down beside me, hands lifting me, and tears fall on me, mixing with mine.

from *Gowie Corby Plays Chicken* by Gene Kemp

Reading for Meaning

1 Why was Gowie Corby fairly cheerful when he arrived at school?

2 What changed his mood?

3 After school, what causes Gowie Corby to feel that something is wrong?

4 How does Gowie get information from Heather?

5 What comments would you make about Gowie's treatment of Heather?

6 Why was Gowie worried about the team?

7 '. . . I am beside her, smiling a face full of teeth like Tom in a Tom and Jerry cartoon.' Why is Gowie behaving in this way?

8 '. . . I am killing myself with laughter inside . . .' Why do you think Gowie is feeling this way?

9 Where does Miss Plum part company with Gowie?

10 What are Gowie's feelings towards Miss Plum?

11 Why was the house next to Gowie's empty?

12 Why was Gowie happy when he reached home?

13 What happened to Gowie as he was opening the front door?

14 Why doesn't Gowie fight back?

15 Why do Gowie's attackers run off?

16 What did you learn about Gowie Corby's character from your reading of this passage?

The Defeat of Fagso

Thirteen-year-old Jimmy Stewart describes his encounter with the angry bully, Fagso.

Fagso was near enough now for me to see that I was the one he was looking at.

'You other kids beat it!' he said. 'It's Stewart I want!'

Joe swallowed, but he stayed beside me. Gladys shouted, 'You're a coward, Fagso Brown! I'll tell the police!'

Midge trembled, 'Let's run!'

I said, 'I'm not running!'

I walked to meet Fagso and stopped a couple of yards in front of him. My feet were apart and I was on my toes.

'What do you want?' I asked him.

'You!' he said.

He didn't stop and he didn't hurry. He just kept on like a tank and when he was close enough he swung his right fist at my face. My head was so clear, my brain so sharp, that I saw everything as if it were in slow motion. I saw the fist coming and I knew what to do. I caught Fagso's wrist in both hands, I spun round and bent forward, at the same time jerking Fagso's arm down. He flew over me and landed on his back in front of me. He was easier to throw than my father was. He was smaller and much lighter and he had no skill in judo, and no idea that I had any. He hit the towpath with a crash that knocked the breath out of him and I laughed when I thought of the time I had spent practising breakfalls. In a flash I saw the faces of the others; Joe's and Bill's comic with wonder; Gladys's shining with worship; Nicker's and Ginger's unbelieving.

In my triumph I tried to be clever. I stood astride Fagso and got a straight armlock on him and he bit the back of my leg so viciously that I yelled and jumped away. There were tears in my eyes and through them I saw him scramble to his feet.

This time he came at me more cautiously, crouching as he came. I had been cool before: now I was cold and confident and I knew what he was going to do. As soon as his right foot lashed up at me I turned my side to him and lifted my right foot so that Fagso's leg jarred into it. I felt his shin grate along the heel of my shoe and I heard the whistle of his indrawn breath when the pain scorched him. But the force of the kick staggered me, and so furious was his animal courage that even the fire in his leg could not stop him. He swung his fist at me again and I ducked, but not quickly enough. It seemed that a club hit me over the ear: that my head exploded in a burst of light. I fell sideways and yet, while falling, my body was taking over from my numbed brain and doing the things that long practice with my father had trained it to do. I fell and rolled and saw

Fagso's boot sweep past me. I rolled again and I was on my feet before Fagso controlled his swinging kick and turned to face me.

I could hear a high piping voice screaming and I knew Gladys was hurling her kid's fury at Fagso. My head was clearing and I was ready for him. He looked a mess. He was scratched and torn and panting. Too many cigarettes were poor preparation for this long fight. He crouched in front of me, watching, waiting, worried and angry. He was baffled and uncertain what I would do. I put my hand up and stroked my swollen ear.

Instantly he leapt at me, reaching out to clutch me, and almost gladly I took a quick step inside his arms, grabbed his leather jacket in both hands, put my right foot in his stomach and rolled backwards with his rush. As soon as my curved back hit the ground I thrust my right leg out straight and catapulted him over me. Against the sky I saw Fagso flying, arms and legs in a tangle, and I heard the splash as he went into the canal and I felt the water rain down over me.

Slowly I turned on to my hands and knees. I was panting and there was bedlam all about me. Joe, Bill and Gladys were dancing and cheering like mad: Molly was trying to look like a rescued maiden: Midge was frightened: Nicker and Ginger were tearing away so quickly that they must have felt certain that they would be tossed after Fagso. They were

afraid. They had seen Fagso, the unbeatable, beaten by a smaller boy and they could not understand. In one instant Fagso's tyranny had ended and he was no longer big enough for them to shelter behind.

Suddenly the shouting stopped and I heard Bill's voice in the silence.

'He can't swim!'

Still on my hands and knees I looked again at Fagso, out in the middle of the canal. His arms were lashing in the air and his face, eyes and mouth wide open, was just below the surface. I saw the water flow into his mouth when he tried to shout and all I heard from him was a drowned gurgle.

Then Joe Belshaw was going through the water like a torpedo. I didn't see him dive into the canal but there he was, planing across the surface. As Fagso sank Joe reached him and drew him up into the air and tried to turn him on to his back. But Fagso struggled. Panic had got him and he grabbed Joe.

'He'll drown our Joe!' Gladys wailed.

But Joe knew how to deal with desperate Fagso. He pushed Fagso's head under and held it there so long that I began to be afraid.

'You'll drown him!' I heard myself shouting. 'You'll drown him, you fool!'

But Joe didn't drown him. He lifted Fagso's head above the surface again and Fagso was quiet, his head lolling on his shoulder. Joe turned him on to his back and ferried him to the bank right in front of me. I looked down on Joe, blowing the water off the end of his nose, and Fagso, with his long hair in wet points clinging like an octopus to his white face.

'Catch 'old of 'im!' Joe gasped at me.

I grabbed Fagso by one shoulder and Bill took the other and together we couldn't haul him up the bank. Gladys took him by the collar and gave a girlish tug. Molly turned her transistor up and said, 'If you don't get him out of that canal he'll be dead.'

Then Joe was beside us, pushing Gladys out of the way, and the three of us hauled Fagso on to the grass at the edge of the canal.

'On his face!' Joe said.

We turned Fagso over so that his head hung down the bank and the water ran out of him.

'Right!' Joe said. 'On his back again!'

Fagso's face was still white and dead.

'I'll give him the kiss of life,' Bill said.

'You won't, Joe said. 'You don't know how to do it. I'll do it. You hold his head up.'

Then Fagso gave a sort of bark and his eyes blinked open. He looked up at the three of us and took a deep breath.

'You OK, Fagso?' Joe asked.

Fagso grunted and sat up. He shook his head, looked up at me and shook his head again. Then he pushed Joe out of the way and climbed slowly to his feet and his boots squelched. He shook himself like a dog and walked along the towpath away from us without a word. His wet jeans were clinging to his legs and he kept combing his hair back with a quick movement of his hand. We watched him go towards Cronton. Somehow he seemed to be smaller. He was a small solitary boy with nowhere to go. He was loneliness in wet jeans and jerkin and I was sorry for him.

from *The Dragon in the Garden* by Reginald Maddock

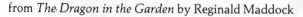

Reading for Meaning

1 How does Joe show that he is a loyal friend of Jimmy Stewart?

2 How does Stewart react to Fagso's presence?

3 'I saw the fist coming and I knew what to do.' What did Stewart do to Fagso?

4 'I stood astride Fagso and got a straight armlock on him . . .' Why was this a mistake for Stewart?

5 How did Stewart know that he had hurt Fagso's leg?

6 'He looked a mess.' Why did Fagso look a mess?

7 What happened to Fagso when Stewart catapulted Fagso over him?

8 '. . . there was bedlam all about me.' Why was there noise and confusion?

9 Why was it obvious that Fagso couldn't swim?

10 What did Joe do when he first reached Fagso?

11 What did panic cause Fagso to do?

12 How did Joe deal with the desperate Fagso?

13 Why did Stewart call out, 'You'll drown him!'?

14 What method did Joe use to get to the bank of the canal?

15 What problem was encountered when Joe and Fagso reached the bank?

16 What happened to Fagso when they turned him over?

17 Why didn't Joe allow Bill to give Fagso the kiss of life?

18 What did Fagso do after he climbed to his feet?

19 What is Stewart's attitude to Fagso at the end of the story?

20 From your reading of the story, what comments would you make about Fagso's character?

POETRY

Monday Blues

Cornflakes were soggy.
Cat licked my egg.
On the school bus
got thumped by Greg.

Sprung again talking
before morning bell —
that Mr Moore can
sure make life hell!

Ticked off for homework —
half out of ten.
Had to miss recess
and do it again.

Strife in mathematics
with Mr Moore.
Sent out to stand in
the corridor.

Looking for battle
came Tracey Frost.
She packs a wallop!
(So guess who lost.)

Biro leaked black ink
on my new jeans.
Soggy fish sandwich
instead of baked beans.

In art and craft room
upset the glue.
Half in my pocket,
the rest in my shoe.

Afternoon playtime,
Shane (my ex-mate)
spread it around that
I fancy Kate.

Practised my footie,
kicked ball quite far.
Guess where it landed?
Mr Moore's car.

Kept in for giggling.
Got home real late.
No wonder bears choose
to *hibernate!*

Robin Klein

Questions

1 What problems did the boy in this poem have at breakfast?

2 What happened to him on the school bus?

3 What happened to him before morning bell?

4 Why did he miss recess?

5 What happened in mathematics?

6 What kind of person was Tracey Frost?

7 What happened to the new jeans belonging to the boy in the poem?

8 What happened in the art and craft room?

9 What happened to Mr Moore's car?

10 Why did the boy in the poem get home late?

11 Why do you think the poem ends with 'No wonder bears choose / to *hibernate!*'?

12 Do you think 'Monday Blues' is a good title for this poem? Why?

Kidnapped!

This morning I got kidnapped
By three masked men.
They stopped me on the sidewalk,
And offered me some candy,
And when I wouldn't take it
They grabbed me by the collar,
And pinned my arms behind me,
And shoved me in the backseat
Of this big black limousine and
Tied my hands behind my back
With sharp and rusty wire.
Then they put a blindfold on me
So I couldn't see where they took me,
And plugged up my ears with cotton
So I couldn't hear their voices.
And drove for 20 miles or
At least for 20 minutes, and then
Dragged me from the car down to
Some cold and mouldy basement,
Where they stuck me in a corner
And went off to get the ransom
Leaving one of them to guard me
With a shotgun pointed at me,
Tied up sitting on a stool. . .
That's why I'm late for school!

Shel Silverstein

Underneath the House

I

It must have been summer,
the time my sister dared me to come underneath the house.
There was a smell of spiders
in the low dirt corridors
and the dark passed our eyes
like a continuous cat making us blind.

We moved on our haunches
breaking cobwebs,
scraping the wall with sticks.
When we heard dulled footsteps
overhead, we held so still I saw our breaths
drift out, looping and falling
losing shape thinly.

In the last room the light
was brown, and the rubble there, once damp for a plant,
now dead as a foot,
dry as an old man's ankle.

II

My father kept his tools under the house;
on a long plank bench were nails and slivers,
boxes and slices of metal
and bits of shattered picture glass and glass-wool padding
to line the gramophone;
over it all the smell of linseed
and the growing spores of crates of mushrooms.

In bed I would listen to the sounds downstairs
of hammering and planing keeping on into the cool hours.
My father with red cedar
dovetailing corners
staining and polishing in small oily circles
or smoothing an edge, the wood hissing,
shavings curling and dropping to the floor.

III

I dream that I run with no shoes
down a cement path
towards a sound and a square of light.
This night is the cylinder
of a brown glass jar;
hands on my head I push up for air.

Rhyll McMaster

Alfie

My brother Alfie's had
his hair cut like a hedge,
it sticks up in the middle
and it's spiky round the edge.

He brushes it each morning
and keeps it fairly clean
you'll see him when he's coming,
he's dyed it bottle green.

Now Alfie thinks he's trendy
he thinks he's really cool
looking like a football pitch
as he walks to school.

All the teachers hate him
because he's got green hair,
and other kids they laugh at him
but Alfie doesn't care.

And I think he's fantastic
I think he's really great,
he's my favourite brother
and I'm his little mate.

David Harmer

Questions

1 Why is Alfie's hair similar to a hedge?

2 How well does Alfie take care of his hair?

3 'You'll see him when he's coming'. Why is this so?

4 What are Alfie's feelings about his hair?

5 In what way is Alfie 'looking like a football pitch'?

6 What is the attitude of the teachers towards Alfie?

7 How do the other kids react to Alfie?

8 How does Alfie feel about their treatment of him?

9 What are the poet's feelings about his brother?

10 Do you think the poet really did have a brother called Alfie? Why or why not?

Number 14

That house you took me to
as a child, with its steps down
from the pavement into a doorway
that smelled of damp, along a passage
into a parlour with a blackleaded grate
and a brace of partridge in white
porcelain, that house
where you grew up under your father's belt —
I pass it every day, and up till now
I have watched the street it stood in
fall to the bulldozers, house by house
each day a bit more sky:
old man, the bulldozers have gone away
but your house is still there
its red front door still saying Number 14
its windows hooded with corrugated iron
jagged against the sky, its time come
and gone, waiting for one more stroke.

Keith Bosley

WRITING

TOPIC SENTENCES

Writers arrange their sentences in paragraphs to make it easy for their readers to understand what is happening. To prevent their writing from rambling, writers relate each of their paragraphs to a certain topic or idea. A paragraph often begins with a topic sentence which indicates what the paragraph will be about.

Now look at the way Betsy Byars describes her character, Carlie, in *The Pinballs*. In each of her paragraphs the topic sentence is in heavy type. Notice how the topic sentence in the first paragraph ('The girl was Carlie') identifies the topic. The rest of the paragraph describes the character of Carlie. The other two paragraphs work in a similar way.

CARLIE

The girl was Carlie. She was as hard to crack as a coconut. She never said anything polite. When anyone asked how she was, she answered 'What's it to you?' or 'Bug off'. Her main fun was watching television, and she threw things at people who blocked her view. Even the dog had been hit with *TV Guide* when he stepped in front of the set when Sonny and Cher were singing 'I Got You, Babe'.

Carlie had to go to the foster home because she couldn't get along with her stepfather. She had had two stepfathers, but the new one, Russell, was the worst. He was mean to everybody in the family, but especially to Carlie. He resented everything she did.

Once he had hit her so hard when she wouldn't tell him where she'd been that she had had concussion. Even with concussion she had struggled up and hit him with a frying pan. 'Nobody hits me without getting hit back,' she had said before she collapsed.

from *The Pinballs* by Betsy Byars

Topic Sentences in Action

Expand three or four of these topic sentences into paragraphs of your own.

- I like food.
- A very unusual face suddenly appeared at the doorway.
- Below us was one of the most beautiful sights we had ever seen.
- My pet, Horace, has some very unusual habits.
- I'm petrified of spiders.
- She was forced to wear a set of horrible dental braces.
- The Headmaster led me into his office.
- It was the worst day of my life.
- One day I'd like to have plenty of money.
- It was the most spectacular sandwich I'd ever made.
- We had never seen an angrier teacher.
- Last night I had the worst dream of my life.
- It was a terrible accident.
- I didn't do it.
- The party was most enjoyable.
- They put me in a dark room without any windows.
- He's one of those people who always irritates others.

LANGUAGE

PROPER AND COMMON NOUNS

Proper nouns can be identified easily because they always start with a capital letter. A proper noun is the name of a *particular* person, animal, place or thing. You come across proper nouns all the time — e.g. Anthony, Debbie, Lassie, New York, February, Monday, Rolls Royce.

On the other hand, a common noun is a general word used for any person, animal, place or thing belonging to a category or class. Most nouns are common nouns — e.g. boy, girl, cat, dog, city, month, day, car, pencil.

Countries and Cities

The names of countries and cities are proper nouns. In the space next to each country, correctly insert from the box the name of its capital city.

Madrid	Rome	Ottawa	Amsterdam
Moscow	Edinburgh	Paris	Tokyo
Athens	London	Stockholm	Washington

Countries	Capital Cities	Countries	Capital Cities
Holland	....	United States	....
Russia	....	Italy	....
Scotland	....	Canada	....
Japan	....	France	....
Sweden	....	England	....
Spain	....	Greece	....

People and Things

Correctly match up the common nouns (people) in the left-hand column with the appropriate common nouns (things) in the right-hand column.

People	Things
journalist	teeth
florist	crime
pilot	flowers
dentist	eyes
chauffeur	plane
musician	newspaper
barber	violin
optician	food
carpenter	hair
teacher	car
detective	wood
chef	blackboard

Proper Nouns in Sentences

Rewrite the following sentences, giving capital letters to the proper nouns.

1 On saturday we will be flying to hong kong.

2 In 1770 captain james cook discovered australia.

3 They decided to remain in italy during january instead of flying to ireland.

4 Ford, toyota and honda are all famous car manufacturers.

5 The ganges is a river flowing through india.

6 The first man to climb mount everest was edmund hillary.

7 The electric lamp and the phonograph were invented by thomas edison.

8 After sir francis drake defeated the spanish armada, queen elizabeth knighted him for his services.

Inserting Common Nouns

In the following statements, the words in italic type are common nouns. Complete each definition by adding another common noun that is suitable.

Example: *Tennis* is a .sport.............

1 An *eagle* is a ....

2 A *cabbage* is a ....

3 *Winter* is a ....

4 A *corgi* is a ....

5 A *piano* is an ....

6 A *lizard* is a ....

7 *Golf* is a ....

8 A *mosquito* is an ....

9 A *rose* is a ....

10 A *hammer* is a ....

11 *Zinc* is a ....

12 An *apple* is a ....

13 *Measles* is a ....

14 A *cent* is a ....

15 A *salmon* is a ....

Matching Up Common Nouns with Proper Nouns

Write down the common nouns in the left-hand column. Then write down the name of the country that belongs to each.

Common Nouns	Proper Nouns
macaroni	Scotland
pyramids	Holland
kilt	Italy
boomerang	Mexico
franc	Russia
igloo	Australia
tulips	Norway
vodka	Egypt
sombrero	India
reindeer	France
turban	Peru
llama	Iceland

PUNCTUATION

THE QUESTION MARK

A question mark (?) is used at the end of a sentence to indicate that a question is being asked. For example:

- What are you doing?
- Is it time to leave?

Sometimes a question mark is the only way of telling a question. Read aloud these two sentences:

- You're arriving tomorrow.
- You're arriving tomorrow?

Using Capital Letters, Question Marks and Full Stops

Correctly punctuate each sentence with the necessary capital letters and a full stop or question mark.

1 who wrote *the pinballs*

2 gene kemp wrote *gowie corby plays chicken*

3 how many novels have you read this year

4 did you enjoy reading *the dragon in the garden*

5 betsy byars wrote *the pinballs* and *the midnight fox*

6 how did harvey break his legs

7 reginald maddock wrote *the dragon in the garden*

8 which novel did you like best

9 fagso is a very unpleasant character

10 when did you finish *the eighteenth emergency* by betsy byars

DRAMA

Hating Alison Ashley

by Robin Klein and Richard Tulloch

Erica Yurken (Erk) feels superior to all the students at her school until Alison Ashley turns up. Alison is not only beautiful, rich and clever, but she is, as well-behaved as a nativity angel. The scene that follows shows what happens when Alison goes to Erica's home to return a pencil case she took by mistake.

CHARACTERS

Alison Ashley   Perfect. Rich, beautiful, clever, well-behaved . . . the sort of person everybody hates.

The Yurken Family

Erica   Ten. A tall flower in a field of couch grass. A hypochondriac and a liar, but destined for a brilliant, glittering career on the stage.

Mum   Likes Bingo, plastic flowers, Parents Without Partners, junk food, dancing and window ornaments like pixies sitting on velvet mushrooms.

Harley   Seventeen. Unemployed (unless lying in a hammock reading books on astral projection counts as employment).

Valjoy   Fifteen. Likes bikies, metal-welding, nail varnish, rude t-shirts, horror movies. Yells a lot and slams doors.

Jedda   Seven. Likes horses, books about horses, horse racing, pony clubs, stables, dressing up as a horse, oats. Utterly embarrassing.

Lennie   Mum's boyfriend. A truckie with a bald patch, a Hawaiian shirt and a great, clanging bumper-bar voice.

Erica's house. Mum enters, with Lennie pursuing her, trying to get a cuddle. Erica watches with disgust.

Erica   Mum?
Mum   Yes, Erk?
Erica   Can I go to Kyle Girls' Grammar next year?
Mum   Kyle Girls' Grammar? With the pale-blue dresses and the little bowler hats and gloves?
Erica   Yes.
Mum   They don't teach you anything there except how to cook for dinner parties and play tennis.
Erica   You can learn ballet dancing.
Lennie   Belly dancing? That'd be good. Come on Erk, do us a belly dance.

(Lennie mimes grotesquely. Valjoy enters.)

Valjoy   Erk, I thought I told you not to wear my slave bangles to school.
Lennie   Erk can be my slave girl any old tick of the clock.
Mum   We're having a barbecue tonight, Erk.

(Jedda cheers.)

Erica   Can't we ever eat anything except junk food?
Valjoy   I won't be here. Spider and Blonk are taking me to the drive-in to see *Claws of Blood*.   *(The doorbell rings.)*   I'll get it. That'll be Spider.

(Valjoy exits. Lennie grabs a squealing Mum and pulls her onto his knee.)

Lennie   Come on, Mum. How about a kiss?
Mum   Oooh, Lennie, you're awful!
Erica   Hear, hear.

(Valjoy returns.)

Valjoy   Erk, there's a kid from your school wants to see you. Can't think why.

(Alison enters.)

Mum   Hello, love, you in the same class as Erk?
Alison   I took home Erica's pencil case by mistake, Mrs Yurken. I thought I'd better return it because of all the homework we've got to do over the weekend.
Mum   Say thank you for the pencil case, Erk. Where's your manners?
Erica   Thanks.   *(Pause)*   Um, Alison, this is my mum, and this is my sister Valjoy and my other sister Jedda and . . .

(She falters to a stop when she gets to Lennie, but he stretches out his hand.)

Lennie   Lennie's the handle. Hey, sweetheart, you're a good-looker. Reckon I'll go back to school. Fillies didn't look like you when I was at school.

Mum   Tell you what, love. We're having a barbecue, so why don't you stay and have tea with us?

(*Erica wills Alison to say 'no'.*)

Erica   Say 'no'! Please Alison, say 'NO'!
Alison   Thank you very much for the invitation, Mrs Yurken.
Mum   Sure your mum wouldn't mind?

(*Erica sends another message.*)

Erica   Yes, she'd hate it! Say you're not allowed!
Alison   Oh no, she wouldn't mind, as long as I get home by dark.

(*Erica is in agony.*)

Mum   Fine! You and Erk might want to play records until tea's ready.
Erica   No! No!
Mum   Erk's just mad about that group Splurge. She plays their album non-stop.
Erica   How embarrassing!   (*Mum, Valjoy and Lennie exit.*)   That's not really true, what Mum said about me liking Splurge. My little sister Jedda's the one who's rapt in Splurge.
Jedda   No, I'm not.
Erica   Yes, you are!
Alison   Was that your dad?

(*Pause*)

Erica   Certainly not!
Alison   I thought he must be your dad because your mother was . . . you know.
Erica   He's a friend of hers. But she really doesn't like him. He's not her real boyfriend or anything. Her real boyfriend's fantastic. He's very handsome and he owns a racehorse stud-farm and a Mercedes.
Alison   Really?
Erica   My real father is dead.
Jedda   I thought he was in Queensland.
Erica   He's dead in Queensland.
Alison   Oh, I'm sorry.

(*Erica pushes Jedda out of the room.*)

Erica   He was killed in a plane crash. He was a test pilot. When he knew his plane was going to crash he flew out over the ocean and crashed there so he wouldn't come down on any houses. Mum never got over it.
Alison   I thought you said she had a boyfriend with a racehorse stud-farm.
Erica   What's that got to do with it? My mum's very popular.

(*Pause*)

Alison   Um . . . Nice house.

Erica   We're only living here because my brother is training to be a missionary. Our
real house is over near Kyle Grammar. Lennie, the man you saw outside, is a
security guard there.

(Jedda enters.)

Jedda   Erk, the barbecue's ready.   *(To Alison)*   Want to hear me call a race?
Erica   No, she doesn't.

(But Jedda launches into it . . .)

Jedda   Irish Mist getting a clear run on the rails, followed by Uranus, King Herod
sneaking up on the outside, followed by Percy Boy, followed by Champagne
Charley, with Sky's the Limit and Take a Gamble well back in the field . . .
Erica   Don't mind her. When Jedda was a baby she was trapped in a burning pram for
several hours.
Jedda   Was I?
Erica   Yes, and if you don't shut up I'll put you back in there.

(Harley staggers into the kitchen in his red underpants.)

Harley   Who's this, Erk?
Erica   This is Alison Ashley. This is my brother Harley.
Alison   Pleased to meet you, Harley. How's school?
Harley   What school?
Alison   Missionary school.
Harley   This is some weird kid, Erk. I don't know what she's talking about.

(Harley exits.)

Erica   They take a vow of silence at missionary school. They're not allowed to mention
it outside the monastery.
Alison   Oh!
Erica   And in case you're wondering, he got a special dispensation from the Pope to
wear red jocks.

(Jedda takes two sausages.)

Mum   Jedda!

*(Mum indicates that Alison hasn't eaten yet. Jedda takes a sausage from her own mouth
and offers it to Alison.)*

Jedda   You want a sausage, Alison?
Alison   Could I have a tissue, please?

(There is a roar of motorcycles outside as Valjoy's friends arrive.)

Valjoy   That's Spider and Blonk.

(Valjoy puts down her plate and jumps to her feet.)

Mum   They're not coming in the house.
Valjoy   Oh, that's not fair, Mum!
Lennie   What's your pick for the fifth, Jedda?
Jedda   Guinea Gold. He always wins on a heavy track.
Mum   Last time Spider washed his leather jacket in the sink without asking.
Lennie   Isn't she cute?
Erica   She sounds like a beery old derelict at the TAB.
Mum   And you're not going out dressed like that!
Valjoy   Get lost!

(Valjoy exits.)

Mum   (*To Alison*)   Do you have any pain-in-the-neck brothers and sisters, love?
Alison   No, there's only me. I'm the only child.

(Lennie shakes up a Coke can.)

Lennie   (*To Alison*)   Watch this. Think quick!   (*He squirts Mum who squeals and giggles.*)   Gets her every time!
Erica   (*To Alison*)   Have some sauce.

(Shouting and revving of bikes outside.)

Mum   (*Yells*)   Will you boys get off to your own homes? If you've got any, which I doubt.
Valjoy   (*Off*)   I'm never allowed to invite my friends home!
Mum   This place is always neck deep in creepy looking tech kids who've been suspended from school.

(Lennie jumps up looking at his watch.)

Lennie   Uh-oh! Time for the big race!

(He grabs a radio and switches it on. A race caller is heard . . .)

Caller   Flashing light is on . . . racing in the Civic Handicap. Himalaya missed the start by a length but the rest got away in a good line. Racing quickly from an outside gate to head them off is Prince Charming, with Cro-Magnon Man settling in behind him and back behind them is Beldale Beauty . . .

Jedda   Sweep, sweep, sweep, sweep!

Mum   It's too late for a sweep, Jedda, the race has started.

(Lennie switches the radio off.)

Lennie   No, I'll turn it off. Here, got the envelopes all made up.   *(Lennie produces them.)*   Come on, everyone pick a horse.

(Jedda and Mum pick slips of paper from the envelope and read the names of their horses.)

Jedda   *(Disappointed)*   Noddy.

Mum   *(Pleased)*   Beldale Beauty.

Jedda   Oh, you've got three there, Mum!

(Mum lays two slips on the table.)

Mum   Cro-Magnon Man for Harley and Devil's Disciple for Valjoy.
Lennie   Come on, Alison, one for you too. Lucky dip.
Alison   Oh, I . . .
Lennie   Got to be in it to win it.

(Alison takes a name.)

Alison   Himalaya.

(Groans from Lennie, Mum and Jedda)

Lennie   That's a roughie, love. Never mind.

(He offers the envelope to Erica.)

Erica   I'm not doing it.
Mum   Oh, come on, Erk, they've started already.

(Lennie picks for her.)

Lennie   Rising Fury for Erk and Prince Charming for me. And they're racing!

(He switches on the radio. All listen, Lennie, Mum and Jedda getting very excited. Alison bewildered but enjoying it, Erica disgusted, but becoming involved as Rising Fury looks like having a winning chance.)

Caller   As they round the home turn, four hundred to run, it's Prince Charming leading them into the straight, half a length from Beldale Beauty with Noddy and Rising Fury ranging up on the outside. Prince Charming is weakening on the turn and is gathered in by Noddy. Rising Fury challenging now . . . Noddy, Rising Fury, Noddy, Rising Fury, anybody's race, but wait, here's a dream split for Himalaya coming from nowhere under the whip. Noddy is gone, Rising Fury just holding Himalaya fifty out, but Himalaya's finishing too well and Himalaya's going to win it! Himalaya by a head from Rising Fury, Cro-Magnon Man took third place with a late run, Prince Charming fourth . . .

(Lennie switches off the radio.)

Mum   Well done, Alison!
Lennie   Boy, you can pick 'em! Have to take you to Randwick some time.
Jedda   What's the prize?
Mum   We forgot to put our money in!
Lennie   Ah, just a bit of fun. Here, Alison, let's say you won the last sausage. How would that be, eh?

(Lennie offers it to Alison.)

Alison   Oh, I've had plenty to eat thank you. I really ought to go, Mrs Yurken.
Lennie   Put it in a doggie bag for you.

(*Lennie wraps it in a tissue and hands it to Alison.*)

Alison   Oh, thank you. And thank you for having me, Mrs Yurken. I've had a very
    nice time.
Lennie   You're a real nice well-behaved kid, Alison.
Mum   You come round any time, love. Erk doesn't get on very well with other kids
    as a rule.
Erica   Mum!
Mum   Erk, get up off your numberplate and say tata nicely.

(*Erica leads Alison to the door. Behind them the scene changes back to the classroom.*)

Erica   Don't take any notice of them, Alison. Valjoy and Lennie and Jedda and that . . .
    they're not really, um . . .
Alison   It's all right, Erk. It's just . . . it's certainly very different from Hedge End Road.
Erica   (*Mimicking*)   'It's certainly very different from Hedge End Road.'
Alison   Erk, I didn't mean . . .
Erica   You snob, Alison Ashley!
Alison   I am not a snob!
Erica   You think you're so great, Alison Ashley! You look down your nose at anyone
    and everyone at Barringa East. You think you're so fantastic, just because you live
    over on Hedge End Road.

Alison   I've got to live somewhere, haven't I?

Erica   How dare you criticise Barringa East! I never even invited you round here in the first place!

Alison   What are you yelling at me for? What on earth did I do, Erk?

Erica   You are the most low-down person I ever met in my life, Alison Ashley! Goodbye!

(Alison runs off, very upset.)

Questions

1 How does Erica feel about having a barbecue?

2 Why has Alison come to Erica's house?

3 What comments would you make about the character of Lennie?

4 'My little sister Jedda's the one who's rapt in Splurge.' Why do you think Erica won't admit in front of Alison that she likes Splurge?

5 '. . . my brother is training to be a missionary.' How do you know that this statement of Erica's is not true?

6 What other untruths does Erica tell?

7 What is unusual about Erica's sister, Jedda?

8 'They're not coming into the house.' Why do you think Mum won't allow Valjoy's friends to come into the house?

9 Why do you think Erica abuses Alison at the end of this scene?

10 What comments would you make about the character of Mum?

11 What comments would you make about the character of Erica?

IT'S MY LIFE

3

AUTOBIOGRAPHIES

Little Ellis and the Boil

At the beginning of his book, *Boy*, Roald Dahl writes, 'Throughout my young days at school and just afterwards a number of things happened to me . . . Some are funny. Some are painful. Some are unpleasant . . . all are true.' The story that follows is painful, unpleasant and true.

During my third term at St Peter's, I got flu and was put to bed in the Sick Room, where the dreaded Matron reigned supreme. In the next bed to mine was a seven-year-old boy called Ellis, whom I liked a lot. Ellis was there because he had an immense and angry-looking boil on the inside of his thigh. I saw it. It was as big as a plum and about the same colour.

One morning, in came the doctor to examine us, and sailing along beside him was the Matron. Her mountainous bosom was enclosed in a starched white envelope, and because of this she somehow reminded me of a painting I had once seen of a four-masted schooner in full canvas running before the wind.

'What's his temperature today?' the doctor asked, pointing at me.

'Just over a hundred, doctor,' the Matron told him.

'He's been up here long enough,' the doctor said. 'Send him back to school tomorrow.' Then he turned to Ellis. 'Take off your pyjama trousers,' he said. He was a very small doctor, with steel-rimmed spectacles and a bald head. He frightened the life out of me.

Ellis removed his pyjama trousers. The doctor bent forward and looked at the boil. 'Hmmm,' he said. 'That's a nasty one, isn't it? We're going to have to do something about that, aren't we, Ellis?'

'What are you going to do?' Ellis asked, trembling.

'Nothing for you to worry about,' the doctor said. 'Just lie back and take no notice of me.'

Little Ellis lay back with his head on the pillow. The doctor had put his bag on the floor at the end of Ellis's bed, and now he knelt down on the floor and opened the bag. Ellis, even when he lifted his head from the pillow, couldn't see what the doctor was doing there. He was hidden by the end of the bed. But I saw everything. I saw him take out a sort of scalpel which had a long steel handle and a small pointed blade. He crouched below the end of Ellis's bed, holding the scalpel in his right hand.

'Give me a large towel, Matron' he said.

The Matron handed him a towel.

Still crouching low and hidden from little Ellis's view by the end of the bed, the doctor unfolded the towel and spread it over the palm of his left hand. In his right hand he held the scalpel.

Ellis was frightened and suspicious. He started raising himself up on his elbows to get a better look. 'Lie down, Ellis,' the doctor said, and even as he spoke, he bounced up from the end of the bed like a jack-in-the-box and flung the outspread towel straight into Ellis's face. Almost in the same second, he thrust his right arm forward and plunged the point of the scalpel deep into the centre of the enormous boil. He gave the blade a quick twist and then withdrew it again before the wretched boy had had time to disentangle his head from the towel.

Ellis screamed. He never saw the scalpel going in and he never saw it coming out, but he felt it all right and he screamed like a stuck pig. I can see him now struggling to get the towel off his head, and when he emerged the tears were streaming down his cheeks and his huge brown eyes were staring at the doctor with a look of utter and total outrage.

'Don't make such a fuss about nothing,' the Matron said.

'Put a dressing on it, Matron,' the doctor said, 'with plenty of mag sulph paste.' And he marched out of the room.

from Boy by Roald Dahl

Reading for Meaning

1 Why was the writer in the sickroom?

2 '. . . Matron reigned supreme.' What does this mean?

3 What was the writer's attitude to Ellis?

4 Why was Ellis in the sick room?

5 The writer compares Ellis's boil to a plum. What does this comparison reveal about the boil?

6 What did the matron remind the writer of?

7 What was the writer's attitude to the doctor?

8 Why do you think Ellis was 'trembling'?

9 How does the doctor try to calm Ellis?

10 What evidence can you find to show that the doctor was deliberately concealing himself from Ellis's view?

11 Why did Ellis raise himself up on his elbows?

12 What did the doctor do with the towel?

13 How did Ellis react to the boil being lanced?

14 'Don't make a fuss about nothing.' What do these words reveal about the matron?

15 What comments would you make about the doctor's treatment of Ellis?

16 Why do you think the writer has so clearly remembered this incident from his childhood?

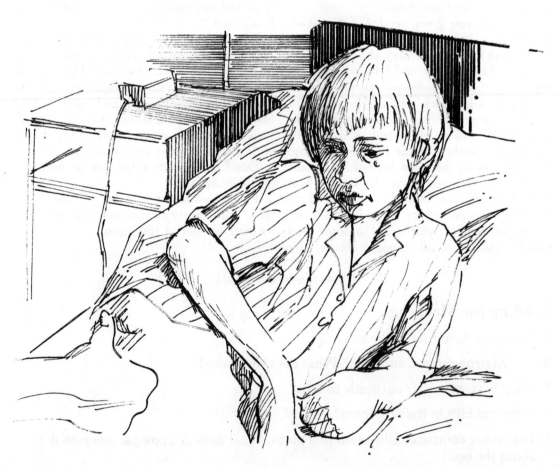

Being Different

Oodgeroo Noonuccal, formerly Kath Walker, is one of Australia's most successful poets. She was the first Aboriginal writer to have poetry published. She was born on Stradbroke Island near Brisbane. Here she describes her early childhood.

As the Twig is Bent

The Childhood Recollections of Sixteen Prominent Australians

Presented by Terry Lane

My father was a ganger of an Aboriginal work gang. The Aboriginals had to do all the dirty work: they were wharfies, roadmakers and drain cleaners. My father was a very straight and determined man, and although he left school at the age of ten to work as a shepherd boy, he was a very learned man. He didn't just leave his learning in the Aboriginal field, but he learned in the white field as well. He was a man who could turn his hand to any darn thing, be it fixing a motor or whatever. He was a very logical man and he bought us toys like iron hoops which he had made by the blacksmith. He taught us how to make shanghais and how to flatten out galvanised iron and sharpen all the edges, making a sharpened square of iron which is marvellous for getting a mullet through the water — *choom!* And he built us tools for the logical reason that we had to bring the food home, so most of our play things were tools.

From my father I learnt about nature and the sea. He loved the sea and I learnt from him how to respect it and not to muck up this old Quandamooka, which is what we called Moreton Bay. Quandamooka is a very beautiful woman but she can also be a very ugly one, and I learnt from my father when to leave her and when to go back to her and how to live in balance with nature. You only took enough food to feed yourself.

I was second-last in a family of seven children and my father, who worked for the government, got three pounds a week plus rations to feed the kids. We'd have died on the rations if we didn't know how to live Aboriginal-style. We belonged to the Noonuccal tribe of Stradbroke Island and although we were receiving a white education we were still receiving the education of Aboriginals on how to survive. We threw all the white man's tucker away. The tapioca — what muck! — we fed to the chooks, and we lived on parrots and bandicoots and dugong and fish and mud oysters, which we call 'quampee'. Dugong tastes smashing. We only took three a year, which was our limit. When you cook dugong it looks like a piece of corner-cut topside, but it's much nicer than that. Our delicacy from the dugong was the bacon which one of the old men used to cure for us. And grumpii sausage, made from the intestine of the dugong, was another favourite. Each family, according to its size, got a piece of the intestine and when the tide was in, my mother used to get us to take it out into the water and play tug-of-war with it. We didn't know it then, but of course we were cleaning it out in the salt water. Then she would boil it, and while the intestine was boiling she would mix the heart, liver and flesh and put herbs from the garden into it and use it to stuff the sausage. She would tie it at the end and boil it again. The Scots call it 'haggis'! It's very, very rich and very beautiful.

Bandicoot tastes like chicken. We all had bandicoot traps. You can't really knock the balance of bandicoots because they breed every month — seven kids a month! They're still on the island in droves, because we no longer eat them. We believed that if we ate them while we had a full belly we'd be punished. That's why we leave the dugong alone now because we feel if we took it now, when we have plenty of white man's food, the good spirit would punish us by taking one of the tribe.

My father was a stubborn man and I think I have inherited that from him. He didn't do much of the rousing around home, Mum did most of that and whenever Mum complained about me roaming around all over the place he used to tell her to leave me alone. 'She's different,' he'd say. I remember the first night he said that. They'd had an argument and I wasn't supposed to be listening. In the end he got really mad and said: 'Leave her alone, she's different.' Mum was complaining because he wouldn't take a hand in chastising me. I was always roaming everywhere and she could never find me. Well, the last thing I wanted to be was different and I really cried myself to sleep that night because I thought my father had deserted me because I didn't know what he meant by 'different'. But he was paying me a compliment I suppose.

When I asked him questions he would say, 'Oh, girl — you're always reaching for the moon. One day you'll get it and it'll turn to cheese in your hand.' That's what he used to say when I'd get him exasperated and he didn't want to answer any more questions.

I was conscious of being a stickybeak. I wanted to know all sorts of things. I remember once bringing in a little golden pig-fish which I had found floating upside down near home. I took a bucket and brought it in and asked if I could keep it. Dad said that it wouldn't live and I asked why not. He told me that it was not made to live on land and that anyway, it was dying. (It had been hurt in the fishermen's nets.) I said: 'He won't die — I'll keep him awake.' And I tried hard to keep it alive, but the next day it was dead. I didn't like my father very much for being right and me being wrong, but it was my first lesson in seeing life and death as it was. That's the way I liked it to be — he never hid anything like that from us.

from *As the Twig Is Bent* edited by Terry Lane

Reading for Meaning

1 What jobs did the Aboriginal workers have to do?

2 '. . . he was a very learned man.' Why does the writer say this about her father?

3 What did the writer's father teach his children?

4 Why did the writer's father build tools for his children?

5 What did the writer learn about the sea from her father?

6 What would have happened if they had not known how to live 'Aboriginal-style'?

7 What did they do with the white man's food?

8 What parts of the dugong did they particularly enjoy?

9 'You can't really knock the balance of bandicoots . . .' According to the writer, why was this so?

10 Why don't they eat the dugong now?

11 Why was the writer's mother complaining to her father about her?

12 What was her father's response to these complaints?

13 Why did the writer consider herself to be a 'stickybeak'?

14 From your reading, what did you learn about the character of the writer's father?

15 What comments would you make about the relationship between the writer and her father?

16 What did you learn about the Aboriginal way of life from your reading of this passage?

Snake Bite

Albert Facey wrote his autobiography, *A Fortunate Life*, when he was in his eighties. The following incident took place over eighty years ago.

After harvest, with the hay and wheat all carted, the burning season was getting near. Frank and I had about eight acres left to clear; the big timber had been burnt down the previous winter and all the small timber and scrub had been chopped to ground level. While waiting for the burning season to open, we were busy clearing a firebreak around the land we intended to burn and clear. This was about half a mile from the house.

Mum had an arrangement to give us an idea when it was lunchtime. She would peg a white tea towel on the clothes line near the house at ten minutes to midday. By the time we got home and had a clean up, lunch would be ready.

One day, at the signal, we started walking towards the house. We were about fifty yards away when we heard Mum let out a terrible scream. She came running out of the lavatory holding up her dress with one hand

and clutching her bottom with the other. She was yelling out loudly, 'I've been bitten by a snake!' Frank and I ran to her and helped her inside the house. Frank took her into the bedroom, and told me to run over to the Connors' place and get Jack to bring his horse and sulky to take Mum to the doctor. It was a little over two miles to Jack's and I ran all the way. It was a very hot day and I was done in when I got there. It took me a few minutes before I could explain what had happened.

Jack wasn't long putting the horse in the sulky and we drove back. Mum was crying when we got there. Frank told Jack that the snake bite was very distinct and he had cut it with his razor and sucked out as much blood as he could.

Mum looked very pale and was badly shocked. After giving me some quick instructions as to what to do while they were away, they set out to get Mum to the doctor in Narrogin as soon as possible. Jack's sulky horse was a beauty, one of the best in the district, and although Frank and Jack were at loggerheads over the boar, they had forgotten about it with the crisis in hand. The trip to Narrogin would take them all afternoon and well into the night.

After they had gone I got a nice handy stick, about four feet long, and went into the lavatory after the snake. This lavatory was mainly used by Mum; I never used it and Frank only sometimes. It was made of galvanised iron and had a small hole cut out at the back to allow Mum to slide the pan in. (The pan was an old kerosene tin cut off to fit.) A bag was hung onto the back wall to cover the hole. With the stick I approached the lavatory, carefully looking in and around, but I couldn't see any sign of the snake. I lifted the bag up very slowly (I was scared stiff), then I heard something move. Quickly I dropped the bag and jumped back. Then all was quiet again. I lifted the bag once more. This time I noticed some feathers, and as I lifted the bag further, more feathers came into view. All at once I knew what had bitten Mum. It wasn't a snake and all my fears turned to mirth. In fact, I almost lost control of myself with laughing.

Mum's snake was a hen. The hen had made a nest close to the pan to lay her eggs and Mum hadn't noticed her. She didn't

mind Mum sitting on the lavatory at first, but when she went broody — a hen can be placid while laying and vicious when broody — she had decided to peck Mum on the bottom.

Mum was very frightened of snakes and also terribly frightened of dingoes. She wouldn't venture outside on her own, except in special circumstances.

They were away for nearly four days. When they came home Mum seemed jolly and didn't show any ill effects from the shock she'd had. I asked her how she was and she said that the doctor had said that he didn't think it was a snake that had bitten her and if it was it wasn't poisonous. She asked if I'd looked around the lavatory for the snake and I said that I had and that I had found the thing that had bitten her. I said that it was still in the lavatory and offered to show it to her.

We went to the lavatory and I lifted up the bag. She looked under and exclaimed, 'Good God. No!' She said that the doctor had said that it looked like beak marks but it never occurred to her that a hen might have done it. She stood for a while and seemed to be thinking, or working something out in her mind. Then suddenly she said, 'Did you have any visitors while we were away or see anyone?' I said, 'No.' 'Well, she said, 'don't you say anything, not even to Frank or anybody about this. If you do I'll be the laughing stock of the district.' She said, 'Bert, I love you, but if you tell anyone about this I'll kill you.' I promised not to tell anyone. Nothing more was said about the 'snake bite'.

from *A Fortunate Life* by A. B. Facey

Reading for Meaning

1 What work was being done by Bert (the writer) and Frank?

2 How did Mum signal to them that it was lunchtime?

3 What happened when they were fifty yards from the house?

4 What did Mum think had happened to her?

5 What did Bert then do?

6 What had Frank done about the snake bite?

7 What was Mum's appearance like?

8 What did Frank and Jack set out to do?

9 What did Bert do after the others had gone?

10 What was the lavatory like?

11 Why did Bert start laughing?

12 Why had the hen bitten Mum?

13 What comments had the doctor made about the bite?

14 Why didn't Mum want Bert to tell anyone about the bite?

15 Did you find this a humorous or serious description? Explain your viewpoint.

POETRY

POEMS ABOUT PEOPLE

Unfortunately this poem is true.

My Best Friend

Maurice was bestest at most things,
At spitting and coughing and burps.
He was good at both running and jumping,
And flipping and pulling girls' skirts.
He was goodest at fighting at playtime.
He was fastest at chasing Ron Pugh —
And if ever he came in down your way,
He was bestest at fighting you too!
He was smashing at swearing and yelling,
He was the best in the class at P.E.,
And when it was time for the cowboys
That Maurice was special to see.
He could shriek like a pig at the butcher's
He could shoot from the hip from afar
But when he came round to the dyin'
Then Maurice was really a star!

He began with a roll of the eyeballs
It went to a twitch of the nose,
And slowly he burbled and staggered,
'til he fell like a dead summer rose.
He'd lie on the ground all-a-twitching,
He'd groan and roll into the road,
And stagger around really awful,
And dribble and holler and moan.
He was bestest at dyin' from arrows,
He'd pretend he'd been shot in the back
And twist all around on the desk tops,
Like someone being stretched on the rack.

He scared all the infants when dyin'.
They thought that it really was true,
For when you saw Maurice a-groaning
Then you thought that it nearly was too!

He was greatest at everything going.
He was super at mucking about,
And making the teachers get angry,
And making the caretaker shout.
He was bestest at swapping — and marbles
At fibbing and talking in class —
But dyin' is what I remember
For dyin' is what he did best.

He died in the years of his thirties,
No arrows or shots in the back
No staggers
No infants applauding —
No bullets or bombers or flak.

He died quite alone in a side ward.
No stabbings and winning of wars
But a quiet caring nurse and a houseman —
No bellows
Or yellings
Or roars.

His dying I'll always remember.
To us it was always a game . . .
For fighting
And falling
And rolling
      And I wish he had kept it the same.

Peter Dixon

Questions

1 Why does the poet say 'Unfortunately this poem is true'?

2 'Maurice was bestest at most things'. What were some of the things Maurice was 'bestest at'?

3 'He was bestest at dyin' from arrows'. Why was this so?

4 Why did Maurice scare the infants with his dying act?

5 What else did Maurice do at school?

6 How did Maurice die in real life?

7 Who looked after Maurice when he died?

8 'His dying I'll always remember'. Why do you think the poet will always remember Maurice's dying?

9 Do you think 'My Best Friend' is a good title for the poem? Why?

10 What were your feelings at the end of this poem?

11 Do you think this poem could have been written from personal experience? Why?

12 Which part of the poem did you like best? Why?

13 Would you like to have had a friend like Maurice? Why?

14 Why do you think the poet wrote this poem?

Who Do You Think You Are?

Who do you think you are and where do you think you came from?
From toenails to the hair of your head you are mixed of earth, of the air,
Of compounds equal to the burning gold and amethyst lights of the
    Mountains of the Blood of Christ at Santa Fe.
Listen to the laboratory man tell what you are made of, man, listen while he
    takes you apart.
Weighing 150 pounds you hold 3,500 cubic feet of gas — oxygen, hydrogen,
    nitrogen.
From 22 pounds and 10 ounces of carbon in you is the filling for 9,000
    lead pencils.
In your blood are 50 grains of iron and in the rest of your frame enough iron
    to make a spike that would hold your weight.
From your 50 ounces of phosphorus could be made 800,000 matches and
    elsewhere in your physical premises are hidden 60 lumps of sugar, 20
    teaspoons of salt, 38 quarts of water, two ounces of lime, and scatterings
    of starch, chloride of potash, magnesium, sulphur, hydrochloric acid.
You are a walking drug store and also a cosmos and a phantasmagoria
    treading a lonesome valley, one of the people, one of the minions and
    myrmidons who would like an answer to the question, 'Who and what are
    you?'

Carl Sandburg

Amanda

Don't bite your nails, Amanda!
Don't hunch your shoulders, Amanda!
Stop that slouching and sit up straight,
Amanda!

(There is a languid, emerald sea,
where the sole inhabitant is me —
a mermaid, drifting blissfully.)

Did you finish your homework, Amanda?
Did you tidy your room, Amanda?
I thought I told you to clean your shoes,
Amanda!

(I am an orphan, roaming the street.
I pattern soft dust with my hushed bare feet.
The silence is golden, the freedom is sweet.)

Don't eat that chocolate, Amanda!
Remember your acne, Amanda!
Will you please look at me when I'm speaking to you,
Amanda!

(I am Rapunzel, I have not a care;
life in a tower is tranquil and rare;
I'll certainly *never* let down my bright hair!)

Stop that sulking at once, Amanda!
You're always so moody, Amanda!
Anyone would think that I nagged at you,
Amanda!

Robin Klein

Bread

My grandmother had craftsman's hands,
stubby and seamed and clay-coloured
with feeling finger-ends.
I often used to perch
upon the kitchen window seat
watching her fisticuff ballooning clouds of dough
then swiftly chop and smack
the pale and swelling loaves-to-be
into their blackened tins,
confer the final benison of her knobbed knuckle-prints
and shove them off to prove themselves
on the warm airing cupboard shelf.
'That's done, my duck,' she'd smile at me,
wiping her floury hands
over her pinafore,
the white dust sifting
on her old black skirt.

Sheila Simmons

THE POET SPEAKS

Hands can be as memorable as faces. My grandmother's hands were ingrained with a lifetime's struggle against dirt from the smoking chimneys of the brickyard where my grandfather was foreman. I can still recall them — plumping up feather beds, throwing grain to her backyard hens, plucking and drawing one of them for Sunday dinner, and, most vividly of all, making her wonderful bread!

In the poem, I am also trying to say something about the way she cherished and encouraged her family — they all did well.

Grandfather

I remember
His sparse white hair and lean face. . .
Creased eyes that twinkled when he laughed
And the sea-worn skin
Patterned to a latticework of lines.
I remember
His blue-veined, calloused hands.
Long gnarled fingers
Stretching out towards the fire —
Three fingers missing —
Yet he was able to make model yachts
And weave baskets.
Each bronzed autumn
He would gather berries.
Each breathing spring
His hands were filled with flowers.

I remember
Worshipping his fisherman's yarns.
Watching his absorbed expression
As he solved the daily crossword
With the slim cigarette, hand rolled,
Placed between his lips.
I remember
The snowdrops.
The impersonal hospital bed.
The reek of antiseptic.

I remember, too,
The weeping child
And wilting daffodils
Laid upon his grave.

Susan Hrynkow

Questions

1 What does the poet remember about her grandfather's hair?

2 Why does the poet remember her grandfather's eyes?

3 What does the poet remember about her grandfather's skin?

4 What does the poet remember about her grandfather's hands?

5 'Yet he was able to make model yachts'. Why does the poet consider this an achievement on the part of her grandfather?

6 Why do you think the poet refers to autumn as 'bronzed'?

7 What did the poet's grandfather do in the autumn?

8 What did the poet's grandfather do in the spring?

9 'I remember/Worshipping his fisherman's yarns'. What does this mean?

10 How did the poet's grandfather behave while he was doing the daily crossword?

11 What does the poet remember about her grandfather dying in hospital?

12 What does the poet remember about the scene at her grandfather's grave?

13 What other suitable title could you give this poem?

14 How do you know that the poet loved her grandfather?

The Old Man's Song

When I was a young man, I followed the gold,
Deep in a mineshaft, all muddy and cold.
Deep in the dark with a flickering light
And never a nugget to gladden my sight —
But it's way, hey! Now I am old,
The mornings were silver, the sunsets were gold.

When I was a young man, I followed the sea.
Cold, wet and shivering often I'd be;
Rocked in the crow's nest or rolled down below
Or sweating my soul out where the Gulf traders go —
But it's way, hey! Now I am old,
The oceans were sapphires, the beaches were gold.

Now I am an old man, I sit in the sun;
Thinking and dreaming of things that I've done.
Remembering laughter, forgetting the pain
And I'd go out and do it all over again —
Way, hey! Lift it along!
What good is your life if it isn't a song?

Bill Scott

Hot Food

We sit down to eat
and the potato's a bit hot
so I only put a little bit on my fork
and I blow
whooph whooph
until it's cool
just cool
then into the mouth
nice.
And there's my brother
he's doing the same
whooph whooph
into the mouth
nice.
There's my mum
she's doing the same
whooph whooph
into the mouth
nice.

But my dad.
My dad.
What does he do?
He stuffs a great big chunk of potato
into his mouth.
then
that really does it.
His eyes pop out
he flaps his hands
he blows, he puffs, he yells
he bobs his head up and down
he spits bits of potato
all over his plate
and he turns to us and he says,
'Watch out everybody —
the potato's very hot.'

Michael Rosen

WRITING

PERSONAL WRITING

The photos and suggestions on the following pages will give you some ideas for writing a few paragraphs about yourself. Before you start, however, you may like to read how the character Gill Ground describes himself.

Me

I guess I was always what is called different, or way out, or a little nuts. Like me or not, that's how it is. Oh, I look like any other eleven-year-old with a thatch of roughly cut brown hair, the correct number of fingers and toes, green eyes that can open or shut with sun or sleep, and a sort of overall foxy face, narrow at the chin. But I have a secret that nobody, not my dead grandmother or Mrs Heister at the orphanage or my various unfortunate teachers, ever guessed. I am ferociously intelligent for my age and at ten I hide this. It is a weapon for defence as comforting as a very sharp knife worn between the skin and the shirt. When a person hasn't money in the pocket, good leather to walk around in, clothes that are his own, and a home address to back him up, I figure he has to have something else — any-

thing. And I'm lucky. I'm not just bright, I'm brilliant, the way the sun is at noon. This is not a boast. It's the truth. It's my gold, my shelter, and my pride. It's completely my profession and I save it like an old miser to spend later. I purposely never learn to spell, which for the simple indicates stupidity. I fall all over my tongue when I am asked to read in school, and when we have a test in arithmetic I dig in the wrong answers very hard with a soft pencil and then smudge them over with my thumb to make it look as though I had tried.

I realise that I sound pretty unsavoury, and maybe if my soft little grandmother had lived longer and I hadn't been thrown into the orphanage the day before I got to be ten I might have chosen to stand and shine.

from *Dorp Dead* by Julia Cunningham

WRITING ABOUT YOURSELF

Using some of the following suggestions, write about yourself under the title 'Me'.

- Looking at yourself in a mirror, describe your physical features.
- What activities do you like doing most?
- What are your dislikes?
- Describe your parents.
- What is your attitude to your parents?
- What clothes do you like wearing?
- Describe your pets if you have any.
- Describe your favourite sport or hobby.
- What jobs do you do around the house?
- What are your favourite television programmes? Why?
- What season of the year do you like best? Why?
- What is your favourite radio station? Why?
- What records do you like playing? Why?
- How do you feel about your brother(s) or sister(s)?
- What places do you like going to?

LANGUAGE

COLLECTIVE NOUNS

A collective noun is a word used for a collection or group of similar persons, animals or things — e.g. herd, army, gang, pack, tribe.

Choosing Collective Nouns

Write down the following sentences and insert the correct collective noun from the brackets in the spaces provided.

1 A .... of aircraft flew over the .... of soldiers. (army, flight)

2 The .... of ships passed the .... of whales. (school, convoy)

3 A .... of spectators watched the .... of cricketers practising.   (crowd, team)

4 An .... of children listened to the .... of singers. (audience, choir)

5 A .... of cattle wandered through the .... of trees. (forest, herd)

6 A .... of wolves attacked the .... of sheep. (pack, flock)

7 A .... of thieves had stolen a .... of stamps. (gang, collection)

8 The actress received a .... of diamonds and a .... of flowers.   (cluster, bouquet)

9 The .... of musicians was given a .... of pups. (litter, band)

10 The .... of directors was entertained by a .... of dancers.   (board, troupe)

Collective Noun Match Up

Correctly match the collective nouns on the left with the people, animals or things on the right.

bunch	cards
tribe	sailors
crew	grapes
pack	natives
library	cars
galaxy	soldiers
staff	books
fleet	stars
troop	teachers

ABSTRACT NOUNS

Abstract nouns are words that name qualities, emotions and actions — e.g. excitement, truth, love, anger, joy, peace. They are things you cannot see or touch.

Working with Abstract Nouns

1 Arrange these abstract nouns in alphabetical order:

horror revenge pride jealousy determination fame delight courage

2 Add the missing letters to form abstract nouns:

a kindn _ _ s

b skilfuln _ _ s

c encouragem _ _ t

d pov _ rt _

e coward _ c _

f stupid _ t _

g freed _ m

h decept _ _ n

i wisd _ m

j friendsh _ p

Identifying the Abstract Nouns

In each group of words there is an abstract noun. Write down the abstract nouns.

1 trumpet laziness chemist

2 executive factory glory

3 sympathy country clerk

4 lawyer importance fruit

5 photo novelist courtesy

6 tooth glamour jockey

7 artist wolf thankfulness

8 determination sky librarian

9 church persuasion carpenter

10 fox astronaut power

Opposites

Write down the abstract nouns in the left-hand column and match them up with their opposites in the right-hand column.

love	failure
bravery	cruelty
success	hatred
strength	cowardice
hope	sadness
honesty	calmness
anger	despair
kindness	ugliness
happiness	weakness
beauty	deceitfulness

PUNCTUATION

THE EXCLAMATION MARK

A sentence or word that expresses urgency, or a strong outburst of feeling or a command ends with an exclamation mark. For example:

- Be quiet!
- Help!
- Fire!

Using the Correct Punctuation Marks

Use an exclamation mark, a question mark or a full stop to end each of the following sentences.

1 Halt

2 Roald Dahl is a famous author

3 Have you read *A Fortunate Life*

4 What an incredible writer she is

5 Where is your copy of *Boy*

6 He's just finished reading *Freaky Friday*

7 Run for your life

8 Which character did you dislike in the book

9 Who is the hero of the story

10 How wonderful

DRAMA

A Soldier at Gallipoli

The playwright, Clem Gorman, has adapted *A Fortunate Life* for the stage. The following scene from the play shows what happened when Australian soldiers landed at Gallipoli. The main character, Bert, appears as a young man during the war and as an old man reflecting on the experience.

CHARACTERS

Young Bert	Soldier One
Old Bert	Soldier Two
Officer	Soldier Three
Voice One	Lieutenant
Voice Two	Soldier
Voice Three	Nurse

Young Bert is writing a letter.

Young Bert 'Dear Grandma. Well, our hour has finally come. There is a calm feeling, all the boys are ready. No one talks much, but we're all wondering where we are, and who we'll be fighting. It's a funny feeling, not knowing. One bloke said we're heading for Turkey, but all the rest of the blokes rubbished him, saying that Turkey wasn't even in the war yet! Do not worry about me, Grandma. I will be alright, and I will look after Roy if I get a chance. Your affectionate grandson, Albert.'

Shortly afterwards, we were told that we were to land on the Gallipoli Peninsula in Turkey.

(The swish of water is heard and the scratch of a match being lit. Whispers begin to be heard as tension builds and dawn gradually arrives.)

Officer Put that match out.
Voice One When'll we get there?
Voice Two Just after dawn, they reckon.
Voice Three Will we go over the side then?
Voice Two I reckon, mate. Unless you'd like to go back to Cairo and check in at the hotel.

(There is a nervous laugh.)

Voice Three   I heard they've got artillery that can knock out a whole ship at one go.
Voice One   Never fear, mate, they're human just like us.
Officer   Stop that whispering, men, and listen. Close to shore you will be met by a small motor boat towing rowing boats. You will climb into the rowing boats and they will take you in to the beach. Then you are to get ashore as best you can and line up on the beach and wait further instructions. Alright, stand by.

(Suddenly a whining sound is heard, then a whoosh! as a shell lands near the ship. All is noise and movement. Rattle of machine-gun and light arms fire. A whistle is blown.)

Alright, men, into the boats!

(There is a rush of men with some shouting and cursing.)

Old Bert   Suddenly all hell broke loose; heavy shelling and shrapnel fire. The ships that were protecting our troops returned the fire.

(As he speaks, Young Bert and several other men mime what he is describing. Darkness is broken by the flash of explosions, the sound of guns, screams of the wounded.)

Bullets were thumping into the rowing boats. Men were being killed all around me. I was terribly frightened. The boat touched bottom and we all waded in to the beach. The Turks had machine guns sweeping our strip of beach. There were many dead already. Wounded men were screaming for help, but we couldn't stop for them. We all ran for our lives over the strip of beach and into the scrub. Men were falling all around me. We were stumbling over bodies, running blind. There wouldn't have been any of us left if we had obeyed that damn fool idea of lining up on the beach!

(After the confusion there is silence.)

When daylight came, we were all very confused. There was no set plan to follow so we formed ourselves into a kind of defensive line, keeping as much as possible under cover from shell fire.
   Our casualties were heavy. We lost many of our chaps to snipers and found that some of these had been shot from behind. This was puzzling so several of us went back to investigate. The Turks were sitting and standing in bushes dressed all in green — their hands, faces, boots, rifles and bayonets were all the same colour as the bushes and scrub. You could walk close to them and not know. We had to find a way to flush these snipers out. What we did was fire several shots into every clump of bush that was big enough to hold a man. Many times after we did this Turks jumped out and surrendered or fell dead.

(Suddenly there is an explosion and a battle scene commences. Bayonets are featured in tableaux.)

It is a terrible thing, a bayonet charge. I was in several in the first few days, in about eleven altogether. You would have to be in one to know what it is like. You are expecting all the time to be hit, and then there is the hand to hand fighting. The awful look on a man's face after he has been bayoneted will, I am sure, haunt me for the rest of my life; I will never forget that dreadful look. I killed men with rifle fire. I was on a machine gun and must have killed hundreds. But there was nothing as terrible as the bayonet.

We continued moving up to the head of what later became known as Shrapnel Gully and kept after the Turks on the hills. The British Navy kept up a continual shelling. On only a few occasions did we get shelled by them.

Eventually, word came that each brigade had been allotted a section of the main firing line. Ours was near a place later to be known and remembered as Lone Pine. At these positions, over the next few days, we managed to get what was left of us into our units and build a proper trenchline. From this time on the fighting changed. It was now trench warfare.

(Pause. Someone is whistling 'Sons of the Sea'. Lights up on Young Bert and some mates in a trench.)

Soldier One   Lice, millions of them. You can't sit still for a minute.

Soldier Two   The only good thing is, it makes us movin' targets for the snipers! Bert here reckons the lice were sent over by the Turks. I reckon they came from home in the Comfort parcels.

Soldier One   I agree with you, Bert, about the food. It definitely comes from the Turks. The meat is saltier than the Red Sea and the bikkies are so hard you have to soak 'em for hours before you can scrape the outside off.

Soldier Two   *(Scraping a biscuit)*   If this biscuit was any harder we could use it for a hand grenade, cop this, Turkey!

(He half stands and mimes throwing a biscuit like a hand grenade at the Turks. There is a burst of fire.)

Murdering swine!

(Pause.)

Soldier Three   *(Nervously)*   I hear they torture their prisoners.

Soldier Two   I'll never let one of them near me!

Soldier One   *(Sniffing)*   Don't worry, mate, you're safe enough.

(Young Bert is opening a parcel.)

Young Bert   Look what I've got. A pair of socks! They've come all the way from Western Australia.

(He peers at the writing on the package.)

Evelyn Gibson, Marine Parade, Bunbury. 'May the soldier who receives these socks come home safely'!

(All gather around.)

Soldier One   I know her. She's a Bunbury lass. And *very nice* too, Bert.

(The soldiers laugh and rib Bert.)

Soldier One   There's one of those pommy Staff Officers on a tour of inspection lads.

(They start to tidy up the trench. Staff Officer and Lieutenant enter.)

Lieutenant   Attention.

(They salute.)

Officer   At ease. What is that terrible smell?

(Soldier Two shuffles.)

Lieutenant   It's the smell of the dead, Sir, in no-man's land.
Officer   Why don't you go out there and bury them.
Lieutenant   Our men would be shot, Sir.
Officer   What's a few men?

(Officer passes along the trenches. They all salute.)

Lieutenant   *(Leaving)*   At ease.
Soldier One   What's a few men? Alright you lot. I'd like you to blow your brains out please.

(The field phone rings. Lieutenant re-enters and answers.)

Lieutenant   Yes, Sir. Yes, Sir. Understood, Sir.

(He hangs up.)

Well what do you know. Armistice to bury the dead. Someone has to go into no-man's land with a white flag. Alright, cover me. If they get me, you can have my share of the lice.

(He fixes a piece of white cloth to a sword and holds it above the sandbags. Then, very slowly, he rises, and makes his way over the top. Young Bert and Solider One watch him go.)

Soldier One   Watchin' him walk across there reminds me of the woolshed dances.
Young Bert   What do you mean?
Soldier One   Walkin' across the floor to ask a girl for a dance!

(They laugh. There is a lighting change. Slowly they stand. Others appear and move over the top. Other soldiers and Turkish soldiers approach. They all smile, shyly, reach

for cigarettes. They hold these positions. The tableau turns into burial party. It is Roy's burial. Young Bert is alone. A Soldier comes to him.)

Soldier   Bert.
Young Bert   Yes, mate.
Soldier   You had better come with me.
Young Bert   What is it?
Soldier   Brace yourself, mate. I've got some bad news for you.
Young Bert   Alright, what is it?
Soldier   It's your brother Roy.

(Young Bert turns away, silently.)

We just got a message. The Officer thought you might want to . . . to see him.
Young Bert   See him?

(Pause.)

Alright. Let's go.

(He follows the Soldier.)

Old Bert   This was a terrible blow to me. I had lost a lot of my mates and seen a lot of men die, but Roy was my brother. We had been through a lot together. I had seen Roy only a few days before. I had been looking forward to seeing him again. I helped to bury him and fifteen other mates who had also been killed on the same day. We put them in a grave side by side on the edge of a clearing they called Shell Green.

(Pause.)

Not long after Roy's death, my part in the Campaign ended. While I was on look-out duty, a shell lobbed into the parapet of our trench and exploded, killing my mate. Several bags filled with sand were blown on top of me — this hurt me badly inside and crushed my right leg. I had difficulty walking or standing upright, and then, while moving to the tunnel to go through to the doctor, a bullet hit me in the shoulder.

(On a hospital ship.)

I was taken across Imbros Bay to a troopship. This ship was badly overcrowded, and we seemed to move very slowly across the sea. We had plenty of time to think that the whole Gallipoli Campaign was a mistake and a terrible, unnecessary loss of life.

(Soldiers are lined up, the injured speaking the following:)

Soldier One   When we were fighting we used to envy those that went away wounded.
Soldier Two   Now I wish I could be back with my mates in the trenches.

Young Bert   Yeah. You feel as if you're betraying them, don't you.
Soldier Three   That's right. After what we've been through together, I feel very loyal to my mates.
Young Bert   That first night on the ship we were all very tired. We didn't need sleeping drugs.

(A Soldier wakes up with a start. A Nurse appears.)

Soldier   What happened? Where are we?
Nurse   You boys didn't sleep; you died. We're in Imbros Harbour. Tomorrow we head back to Egypt.
Old Bert   Now we became nervous again. We knew that many ships had been sunk by submarines in these waters. After all we'd been through, we couldn't bear to think of being sunk on our way home. For a day and a night we travelled on full alert. All lights were out. Men were allowed to speak only in whispers.

(Behind, in the gloom, men light fags, whisper, and wait, wearing lifejackets. A man starts screaming incoherently, starting up. His eyes staring, he is groaning and crying. Young Bert and others rush at him, put their hands over his mouth, hold him down.)

Young Bert   There there, old mate, take it easy, you'll be right as rain soon. When we get to Cairo, mate, there'll be rose gardens and fountains and a thirty piece band, playin' just for us.

(Pause.)

Old Bert   That night is something none of us will ever forget.

(Slow fade to black and silence.)

We arrived at the Port of Alexandria just before noon on the 29th August. I was sent to a converted sports arena called Luna Park, where they looked after us very well. I had my 21st birthday there but didn't tell anyone. It was shortly after this that I received word that my elder brother Joseph had been killed at Gallipoli. He was found with several bayonet wounds in him.

Young Bert   About four weeks later after being given lengthy examinations and answering a lot of questions, I was told that my wounds had healed but the board wasn't satisfied with my condition. I was still suffering faintness and internal pain, and vomiting blood — the cause of this had the doctors baffled. They recommended that I be sent to England or Australia for six months further treatment and observation. They asked me to choose and I chose Australia.

Old Bert   I had been on Gallipoli only six days short of four months.

from *A Fortunate Life* — *The Play* by Clem Gorman

Questions

1 What does Bert tell his grandmother in his letter?

2 'Put that match out.' Why do you think the officer gives this order?

3 'Suddenly all hell broke loose.' What causes Bert to say this?

4 Why couldn't they stop to help the wounded?

5 How did they flush out the snipers?

6 According to Bert, why was a bayonet charge 'a terrible thing'?

7 What problems did the Australian soldiers have with the food?

8 Why didn't the soldiers bury their dead lying in no-man's land?

9 'What's a few men?' What comments would you make about the character of this officer?

10 What happened to Bert's brother, Roy?

11 How was Bert wounded?

12 What were Bert's feelings about the Gallipoli Campaign?

13 How did Bert feel about leaving his mates behind?

14 What happened to Bert's elder brother, Joseph?

15 What was Bert's physical condition like at the end of this scene?

16 What did you learn about Bert's character from your reading of this scene?

17 What evidence can you find to show that this was a real-life experience?

18 What problems would you have in performing this scene on stage?

ANIMALS

4

NOVELS

The Baby Fox

In this passage from *The Midnight Fox* we share Tom's emotions as he experiences the danger of the black fox and her cub.

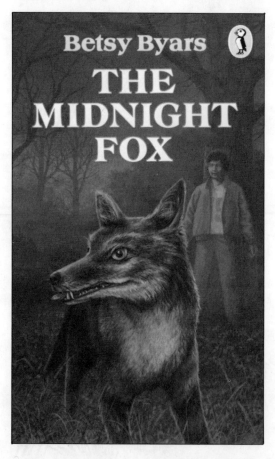

It seemed to get dark quickly that night. Uncle Fred was already out on the back porch. He had brought out a chair and was sitting with his gun beside him, pointing to the floor. I never saw anyone sit any quieter. You wouldn't have noticed him at all he was so still.

I stood behind him inside the screen door. Through the screen I could see the tiny fox lift his black nose and cry again. Now, for the first time, there was an answer — the bark of his mother.

I looked towards the garden, because that's where the sound had come from, but Uncle

Fred did not even turn his head. In a frenzy now that he had heard his mother, the baby fox moved about the cage, pulling at the wire and crying again and again.

Just then there was the sound of thunder from the west, a long rolling sound, and Aunt Millie came to the door beside me and said, 'Bless me, is that thunder?' She looked out at the sky. 'Was that thunder, Fred?'

'Could be,' he said without moving.

'Look!' Aunt Millie said, 'I swear I see black clouds. You see, Tom?'

'Yes'm.'

'And feel that breeze. Honestly, when you think you have reached absolutely the end of your endurance, then the breeze comes. I could not have drawn one more breath of hot air, and now we are going to have a storm.'

We stood in the doorway, feeling the breeze, forgetting for a moment the baby fox.

Then I saw Uncle Fred's gun rise ever so slightly in the direction of the fence behind the garage. I could not see any sign of the fox, but I knew that she must be there. Uncle Fred would not be wrong.

The breeze quickened, and abruptly the dishpan which Aunt Millie had left on the porch railing clattered to the floor. For the

first time Uncle Fred turned his head and looked in annoyance at the pan and then at Aunt Millie.

'Did it scare your fox off?' she asked.

He nodded, then shifted in the chair and said, 'She'll be back.'

In just this short time the sky to the west had gotten black as ink. Low on the horizon forks of lightning streaked the sky.

'Now, Fred, don't you sit out here while it's thundering and lightning. I mean it. No fox is worth getting struck by lightning for.'

He nodded and she turned to me and said, 'You come on and help me shut the windows. Some of those upstairs are stuck wide open. Just hit them with the heel of your hand on the side till you can get them down.'

I started up the stairs and she said again, 'Fred, come on in when it starts storming. That fox'll be back tomorrow night too.'

I went upstairs and started hitting the sides of the windows. I had just gotten one window to jerk down about two inches when I heard the gunshot. I had never heard any worse sound in my life. It was a very final sound, like the most enormous period in the world. Bam. Period. The end.

I ran out of my room and down the steps so fast I could not even tell you how many times my feet touched the stairs, none

maybe. I went out the back door, opening it so fast I hit the back of Uncle Fred's chair. I looked towards the rabbit hutch, said, 'Where?' then looked at the back fence. Then I looked down at Uncle Fred, who was doing something with his gun.

'Missed,' he said.

Suddenly I felt weak. My legs were like two pieces of rope, like that trick that Hindu magicians do when they make rope come straight up out of a basket and then say a magic word and make the rope collapse. My legs felt like they were going to collapse at any second. I managed to force these two pieces of rope to carry me up the stairs and into the room.

I closed two windows, and the third one, in sympathy perhaps, just banged down all by itself. Then I sank to the bed.

from *The Midnight Fox* by Betsy Byers

Reading for Meaning

1 What was unusual about the way Uncle Fred was sitting on the porch?

2 Standing behind Uncle Fred, what could the storyteller see?

3 What effect did the bark of the baby fox's mother have on Uncle Fred?

4 Why was the baby fox in a frenzy?

5 Why did the storyteller believe that the fox must be near the fence behind the garage?

6 How did the dishpan's clattering to the floor affect Uncle Fred?

7 Why didn't Aunt Millie want Uncle Fred to sit out on the porch?

8 Why did the storyteller go upstairs?

9 How did the storyteller feel about the gunshot?

10 What did the storyteller do after hearing the gunshot?

11 What evidence can you find to show that the storyteller moved very fast to the back porch?

12 'Suddenly I felt weak.' Why do you think the storyteller felt weak?

13 What did you learn about the character of the storyteller from this incident?

14 What were your feelings towards Uncle Fred?

15 Did you enjoy reading this passage? Why or why not?

Mrs Frisby, the Crow and the Cat

Mrs Frisby, the head of a family of field mice, shows great bravery in saving the life of Jeremy, a young crow.

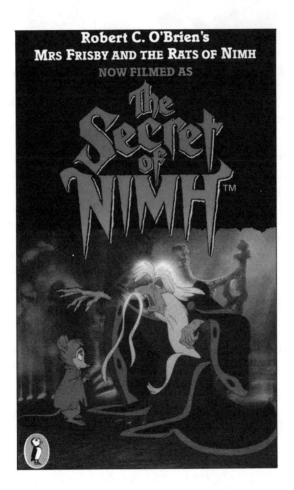

When at length she came abreast of the barn, she saw the wire fence that marked the other end of the pasture; and as she approached it, she was startled by a sudden outburst of noise. She thought at first it was a hen, strayed from the chickenyard — caught by a fox? She looked down the fence and saw that it was no hen at all, but a young crow, flapping in the grass, acting most oddly. As she watched, he fluttered to the top wire of the fence, where he perched nervously for a moment. Then he spread his wings, flapped hard, and took off — but after flying four feet he stopped with a snap and crashed to the ground again, shedding a flurry of black feathers and squawking loudly.

He was tied to the fence. A piece of something silvery — it looked like wire — was tangled around one of his legs; the other end of it was caught in the fence. Mrs Frisby walked closer, and then she could see it was not wire after all, but a length of silver-coloured string, probably left over from a Christmas package.

The crow was sitting on the fence, pecking

ineffectively at the string with his bill, caw-
ing softly to himself, a miserable sound.
After a moment he spread his wings, and she
could see he was going to try to fly again.

'Wait,' said Mrs Frisby.

The crow looked down and saw her in the
grass.

'Why should I wait? Can't you see I'm
caught? I've got to get loose.'

'But if you make so much noise again the
cat is sure to hear. If he hasn't heard already.'

'You'd make a noise, too, if you were tied
to a fence with a piece of string, and with
night coming on.'

'I would not,' said Mrs Frisby, 'if I had any
sense and knew there was a cat near by. Who
tied you?' She was trying to calm the crow,
who was obviously terrified.

He looked embarrassed and stared at his
feet. 'I picked up the string. It got tangled
with my foot. I sat on the fence to try to get
it off, and it caught on the fence.'

'Why did you pick up the string?'

The crow, who was very young indeed —
in fact, only a year old — said wearily.
'Because it was shiny.'

'You knew better.'

'I had been told.'

Birdbrain, thought Mrs Frisby, and then
recalled what her husband used to say: The
size of the brain is no measure of its capacity.
And well she might recall it, for the crow's
head was double the size of her own.

'Sit quietly,' she said. 'Look towards the
house and see if you see the cat.'

'I don't see him. But I can't see behind the
bushes. Oh, if I could just fly higher . . .'

'Don't,' said Mrs Frisby. She looked at the
sun; it was setting behind the trees. She
thought of Timothy, and of the medicine she
was carrying. Yet she knew she could not
leave the foolish crow there to be killed —
and killed he surely would be before sunrise
— just for want of a few minutes' work. She
might still make it by dusk if she hurried.

'Come down here,' she said. 'I'll get the
string off.'

'How?' said the crow dubiously.

'Don't argue. I have only a few minutes.'
She said this in a voice so authoritative that
the crow fluttered down immediately.

'But if the cat comes . . .' he said.

'If the cat comes, he'll knock you off the
fence with one jump and catch you with the
next. Be still.' She was already at work with
her sharp teeth, gnawing at the string. It was
twined and twisted and twined again around
his right ankle, and she saw she would have
to cut through it three times to get it off.

As she finished the second strand, the
crow, who was staring towards the house,
suddenly cried out:

'I see the cat!'

'Quiet!' whispered Mrs Frisby. 'Does he see
us?'

'I don't know. Yes. He's looking at me. I
don't think he can see you.'

'Stand perfectly still. Don't get in a panic.'
She did not look up but started on the third
strand.

'He's moving this way.'

'Fast or slow?'

'Medium. I think he's trying to figure out what I'm doing.'

She cut through the last strand, gave a tug, and the string fell off.

'There, you're free. Fly off, and be quick.'

'But what about you?'

'Maybe he hasn't seen me.'

'But he will. He's coming closer.'

Mrs Frisby looked around. There was not a bit of cover anywhere near, not a rock nor a hole nor a log; nothing at all closer than the chicken yard — and that was in the direction the cat was coming from, and a long way off.

'Look,' said the crow. 'Climb on my back. Quick. And hang on.'

Mrs Frisby did what she was told, first grasping the precious packages of medicine tightly between her teeth.

'Are you on?'

'Yes.'

She gripped the feathers on his back, felt the beat of his powerful black wings, felt a dizzying upward surge, and shut her eyes tight.

'Just in time,' said the crow, and she heard the angry scream of the cat as he leaped at where they had just been. 'It's lucky you're so light. I can scarcely tell you're there.' Lucky indeed, thought Mrs Frisby; if it had not been for your foolishness I'd never have got into such a scrape. However, she thought it wise not to say so, under the circumstances.

'Where do you live?' asked the crow.

'In the garden patch. Near the big stone.'

'I'll drop you off there.' He banked alarmingly, and for a moment Mrs Frisby thought he meant it literally. But a few seconds later — so fast does the crow fly — they were gliding to earth a yard from her front door.

'Thank you very much,' said Mrs Frisby, hopping to the ground.

'It's I who should be thanking you,' said the crow. 'You saved my life.'

'And you mine.'

'Ah, but that's not quite even. Yours wouldn't have been risked if it had not been for me — and my piece of string.' And since this was just what she had been thinking, Mrs Frisby did not argue.

'We all help one another against the cat,' she said.

'True. Just the same, I am in debt to you. If the time ever comes when I can help you, I hope you will ask me. My name is Jeremy. Mention it to any crow you see in these woods and he will find me.'

'Thank you,' said Mrs Frisby, 'I will remember.'

from *Mrs Frisby and the Rats of Nimh* by Robert C. O'Brien

Reading for Meaning

1 Why was Mrs Frisby startled as she approached the wire fence?

2 Why did the young crow appear to be acting oddly?

3 Why couldn't the crow fly away from the fence?

4 Why, according to Mrs Frisby, was it dangerous for the crow to make any more noise?

5 How had the crow become tied to the fence?

6 Why had the crow picked up the string?

7 What did Mrs Frisby think would happen to the crow if she left him?

8 How did Mrs Frisby get the string off the crow's foot?

9 When did the crow see the cat?

10 Why didn't the crow fly off immediately he was free?

11 'Climb on my back. Quick.' Why does Mrs Frisby obey the crow?

12 Explain how Mrs Frisby and the crow had a narrow escape from the cat?

13 Why did the crow have no trouble in carrying Mrs Frisby?

14 Why was, Jeremy, the young crow, in debt to Mrs Frisby?

15 What human qualities did Mrs Frisby reveal in this passage?

Rontu, the Wonder Dog

Karana's dog, Rontu, is fortunate to escape with his life when he encounters some wild dogs, face to face.

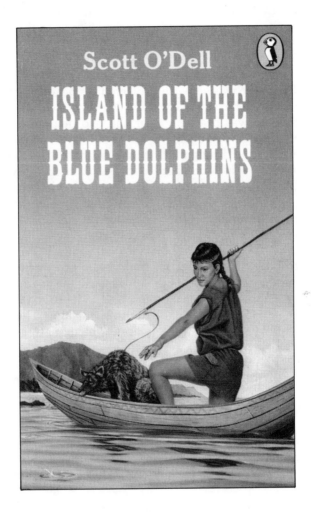

I heard the sound of dogs fighting. The sound came from far off, perhaps from the ravine, and taking my bow and arrows, I hurried in that direction.

I went down the path which led to the spring. There were tracks of the wild dogs around the spring, and among them I saw the large ones of Rontu. The tracks led away through the ravine which winds to the sea. I heard again the distant sound of fighting.

I went slowly through the ravine because of my bow and arrows.

At last I came to the place where it opens into a meadow right at the edge of a low sea cliff. Sometimes in the summers, a long time ago, my people had lived here. They gathered shellfish on the rocks and ate them here, leaving the shells which after many summers had formed a mound. Over this grass had grown, and a thick-leaved plant called *gnapan*.

On this mound, among the grasses and the plants, stood Rontu. He stood facing me, with his back to the sea cliff. In front of him in a half-circle were the wild dogs. At first I thought that the pack had driven him there against the cliff and were getting ready to attack him. But I soon saw that two dogs stood out from the rest of the pack, between it and Rontu, and that their muzzles were wet with blood.

One of these dogs was the leader who had taken Rontu's place when he had come to live with me. The other one, which was spotted, I had never seen. The battle was between Rontu and these two dogs. The rest were there to fall upon whichever was beaten.

So great was the noise made by the pack, they had not heard me as I came through the brush, nor did they see me now as I stood at the edge of the meadow. They sat on their haunches and barked, with their eyes fixed on the others. But I was sure that Rontu knew I was somewhere near, for he raised his head and smelled the air.

The two dogs were trotting back and forth along the foot of the mound, watching Rontu. The fight had probably started at the

spring and they had stalked him to this place where he had chosen to fight.

The sea cliff was behind him and they could not reach him from that direction so they were trying to think of some other way. It would have been easier if one could have attacked him from the back and one from the front.

Rontu did not move from where he stood on top of the mound. Now and again he lowered his head to lick a wound on his leg, but whenever he did he always kept his eyes on the two dogs trotting up and down.

I could have shot them, for they were within reach of my bow, or driven off the pack, yet I stood in the brush and watched. This was a battle between them and Rontu. If I stopped it, they would surely fight again, perhaps at some other place less favourable to him.

Rontu again licked his wound and this time he did not watch the two dogs moving slowly past the mound. I thought it was a lure and so it proved to be, for suddenly they ran towards him. They came from opposite sides of the mound, ears laid back and teeth bared.

Rontu did not wait for the attack, but, leaping at the nearer one, turned his shoulder and with his head lowered caught the dog's foreleg. The pack was quiet. In the silence, I

could hear the sound of the bone breaking, and the dog backed away on three legs.

The spotted dog had reached the top of the mound. Whirling away from the one he had crippled, Rontu faced him, but not in time to fend off the first heavy rush. Teeth slashed at his throat and, as he turned his body, struck him instead on the flank, and he went down.

At that moment, while he lay there on the grass with the dog circling warily and the pack moving slowly towards him, without knowing that I did so, I fitted an arrow to the bow. A good distance separated Rontu from his attacker and I could end the battle before he was wounded further or the pack fell upon him. Yet, as before, I did not send the arrow.

The spotted dog paused, and turned in his tracks, and again leaped, this time from behind.

Rontu was still lying in the grass with his paws under him and I thought he did not see that the other was upon him. But crouching there, he suddenly raised himself and at the same time fastened his teeth in the dog's throat.

Together they rolled off the mound, yet Rontu did not let go. The pack sat restless in the grass.

In a short time Rontu rose to his feet and left the spotted dog where it lay. He walked to the top of the mound and lifted his head and gave a long howl. I had never heard this sound before. It was the sound of many things that I did not understand.

He trotted past me and up the ravine. When I got to the house he was there waiting, as if he had not been away or nothing had happened.

from *Island of the Blue Dolphins* by Scott O'Dell

Reading for Meaning

1 Where did the sound of dogs fighting seem to be coming from?

2 Why did the storyteller, Karana, proceed slowly through the ravine?

3 How had the mound been formed?

4 What would happen to the dog that was defeated?

5 Why had the pack not heard Karana as she came through the brush?

6 Why did she think that Rontu was aware of her presence?

7 Why couldn't the dogs attack Rontu from behind?

8 Why didn't Karana stop the dog fight?

9 How did the two dogs begin their attack on Rontu?

10 What did Rontu do to the nearer dog?

11 What did the spotted dog do after he had reached the top of the mound?

12 Why do you think Karana fitted an arrow to her bow?

13 How did Rontu finally kill the spotted dog?

14 What did Rontu do just after he left the spotted dog?

15 When Karana reached the house, how did Rontu behave?

POETRY

ANIMAL PAIRS

My Dog

My dog is a mongrel.
Half this,
Quarter that,
And a bit of most things,
But he's mine;
He likes me.
His eyes sparkle
When he runs,
He barks
At the baker,
Bites the postman,
Growls at insurance
And pants when the butcher
Stamps at the door.
His teeth are white,
Sharp and slobbery;
He smiles
When I smile at him,
Droops when
I am angry.
His coat prickles
At all angles;
His ears are odd,
His tongue lolling,
His tail a wavering banner.
He sleeps in a box
In my room
And scratches.
When everyone is
Loathsome,
There is him.

Joan Tate

Questions

1 What does the poet tell you about her dog's breeding?

2 Why do you think the poet says 'But he's mine'?

3 How does the dog react to the baker?

4 Why do you think the dog 'pants' when the butcher arrives?

5 Why do you think the poet refers to the dog's teeth as 'slobbery'?

6 What does the dog do when the poet smiles at him?

7 What does the dog do when the poet is angry?

8 What is the meaning of 'His tail a wavering banner'?

9 What evidence can you find to show that the dog is not handsome?

10 What do you think the poet means when she says: 'When everyone is/ Loathsome,/ There is him.'

11 Would you like to own a dog like this one? Why or why not?

The Country Dog

The country dog with his eager grin
Enjoys the sound of the market din.
　　To a city dog, he's a noisy clown,
　　He likes a scrap when he comes to town.

The rushing road and the traffic's beat
He sits up straight in the wide front seat.
　　He likes the seat of a country car
　　His head stuck out where the breezes are.

He likes the run of the open land
Where the creekbeds wind and the big trees stand.
　　By the shining dam with its local frog,
　　With one ear cocked, goes the country dog.

By tractor seat or the furrow's line
He'll sit and wait for his master's sign.
　　With tireless paw and a bark or yelp
　　He runs the farm with the farmer's help.

There's a paddock lunch with the watching crows
But the country dog each wise bird knows.
　　The hours will dustily drift away
　　And there comes an end to a dog's long day.

The restless sheep on the ranges cry
The weary wind for the dawn will sigh
     The small flames drowse on the old bush log
     And light the dreams of the country dog.

Max Fatchen

Questions

1 Why do you think a city dog would consider the country dog 'a noisy clown'?

2 What does the country dog like when he comes to town?

3 Why does the poet refer to the road as 'rushing'?

4 What does the country dog do while sitting in the wide front seat of the car?

5 Why do you think the poet describes the dam as 'shining'?

6 What is the meaning of 'He'll sit and wait for his master's sign'?

7 What does the country dog do to help the farmer?

8 What does the country dog do at night?

9 Think of another title for this poem.

10 What does this poem show you about the life of the country dog?

The Mad Yak

I am watching them churn the last milk
    they'll ever get from me.
They are waiting for me to die;
They want to make buttons out of my bones.
Where are my sisters and brothers?
That tall monk there, loading my uncle,
    he has a new cap.
And that idiot student of his —
I never saw that muffler before.
Poor uncle, he lets them load him.
How sad he is, how tired!
I wonder what they'll do with his bones?
And that beautiful tail!
How many shoelaces will they make of that!

Gregory Corso

The Yak

As a friend to the children, commend me the yak;
You will find it exactly the thing:
It will carry and fetch, you can ride on its back,
Or lead it about with a string.

The Tartar who dwells in the plains of Tibet
(A desolate region of snow),
Has for centuries made it a nursery pet,
And surely the Tartar should know!

Then tell your papa where the yak can be got,
And if he is awfully rich,
He will buy you the creature — or else he will not.
I cannot be positive which.

Hilaire Belloc

The Death of a Cat

I rose early
On the fourth day
Of his illness,
And went downstairs
To see if he was
All right.
He was not in the
House, and I rushed
Wildly round the
Garden calling his name.
I found him lying
Under a rhododendron
Bush,
His black fur
Wet, and matted
With the dew.
I knelt down beside him,
And he opened his
Mouth as if to
Miaow
But no sound came.

I picked him up
And he lay quietly
In my arms
As I carried him
Indoors.
Suddenly he gave
A quiet miaow
And I felt his body tense
And then lie still.
I had his warm
Lifeless body on
The floor, and
Rubbed my fingers
Through his fur.
A warm tear
Dribbled down
My cheek and
Left a salt taste
On my lips.
I stood up, and
Walked quietly
Out of the room.

Anthony Thompson

Questions

1 Why did the poet go downstairs early?

2 Why did the poet rush wildly around the garden?

3 Where did the poet find his cat?

4 What had happened to the cat's fur?

5 What did the cat do when the poet knelt down beside him?

6 What did the poet then do with his cat?

7 What did the cat do just before it died?

8 What did the poet do to his cat after it died?

9 How do you know that the poet was very sad when his cat died?

10 What did you learn about the character of the poet from your reading of this poem?

One Gone, Eight to Go

On a night of savage frost,
This year, my smallest cat,
The fluffy one, got lost.
And I thought that that was that.

Until, late home, I heard,
As I fumbled for my key,
The weak sound of some bird.
He was there, mewing to me.

There, on the icy sill,
Lifting his crusted head,
He looked far worse than ill.
He looked, I'd say, quite dead.

Indoors, though, he could eat,
And he showed, and fluffed his tail.
So much for a plate of meat.
So much for a storm of hail.

Now, by the burning grate,
I stroke his fragile spine,
Thinking of time, and fate.
Lives go. Men don't have nine,

As kittens do, to waste.
This lucky one survives,
And purrs, affronted-faced.
But even he, who thrives

Tonight, in my cupped hands,
And will grow big and grey,
Will sense, in time, the sands,
And fail, and shrink away.

George Macbeth

Frogs

for Elizabeth Scott

Fat frogs squat greenly
in waterholes.
Swim with hind legs
on hinges.

They sleep all day
under tankstands
where damp fern fronds
hang in fringes.

But on blowy nights
when rain rattles
on the stiff leaves
of palm and mango,

they swell their throats,
bellow, honk and tinkle —
that's what I call
a frog fandango.

Bill Scott

Frog

Under the bushes
sleek and slim
there's a middling frog.
I look for him
carefully, turning
stone by stone;
often I find him
quite alone
where the grass is specially
sharp and thin,
and the tangled ivy
closes in,
and the world is shadowed
in green and grey . . .
He hasn't got anything
much to say,
but his throat moves silently
as though
there were something I certainly
ought to know;
then he flicks his tongue
like a needle, where
the small gnats twirl
in the misty air.
He sometimes jumps.
He sometimes goes
wimbling wambling . . .
I suppose
a frog is a slithery
thing to be.
I wonder whatever
he thinks of ME?

Jean Kenward

WRITING

DESCRIBING ANIMALS

Read through the following two passages. Observe how the writers describe the physical appearance and behaviour of the fox and the hippopotamus.   •

The Red Fox

He was four years old, and he had never found a mate. He was long legged, lean flanked. His paws were black, his underbelly flushed with cream and the long fur on the rest of his body was a flaunting arrogant copper red, tainted with rust. Under his brush his long thick hairs were creamy white. His prick ears were black tipped, his glowing eyes were black rimmed, and his stiff whiskers were white.

He had been born in a thunderstorm, and the whole of his life since had been stormy. He learned, swiftly and terribly, that his chief enemies were men. Men, thundering on their stampeding horses, crashing over the ground, yelling and shouting, whips flailing, red mouths gaping as they shrieked yoick and tally-ho and yip, yip, yip, or their horns sounded the Gone Away or the Gone to Earth or the View-Halloo.

He knew that it was men who sent the racing hounds, the pack belling its bloodlust as it marked his trail, following his scent, running headlong on his track.

He knew that the hounds had torn his mother apart; he knew that men had come to the earth and sent down the terriers and pulled out his brother and two sisters and killed them too. He had been playing when the men came, and he had learned his lesson well. He froze, a red stone against the ground; a red pebble, a rounded rock, so still that nothing saw him and nothing scented him and the men went away, not knowing he was there.

He crept away that night, afraid to linger. There was blood-smell on the grass, fear-smell in the trees, and the thin drear rain that wetted him echoed his sorrow.

He was not very old and he was very lonely. He played with a stick, but it would not lie and pounce and bite and butt. He tried to play with a frog but it squealed and jumped into the water. He bruised his nose on the rolling hedgehog that armoured its body with spikes, hiding its soft parts from him.

He learned to hunt and he learned to kill. He learned that hounds could not track through water; they could not follow when his paws were soiled with cattle dung; they could not slide, as he could, through a narrow drain, and race down the hillside and leap into a tree. He lay along the branch, watching the hunt go by, and his scent blew into the air and away, never betraying his presence.

He knew where the geese fattened on the

summer pools. He knew where the baby rabbits chased under the hunting moon. Night after night when he was full fed and comfortable and almost asleep, he lay with his nose on his paws and watched the moon running, speeding away from the shaggy grey cloud beasts as he ran from the pelting hounds.

from *The Fox at Drummers' Darkness* by Joyce Stranger

Thinking about the Writer's Technique

1 The writer uses a number of colours to describe the fox. What are these colours? What parts of the fox's body do they describe? Which colour do you think stands out the most?

2 What sound words does the writer use to suggest the noises made by the men on horses?

3 What feelings do you have towards the men? Why?

4 How does the writer cause you to feel sorry for the fox?

5 Do you think this is a good description of the fox and its life? Why or why not?

The Hippo

Gradually we rounded the bend of the river, and there, about three hundred yards ahead of us on the opposite shore, lay the white bulk of the sandbank, frilled with ripples. The old man gave a grunt of relief at the sight, and started to paddle more swiftly.

'Nearly there,' I said gaily, 'and not a hippo in sight.'

The words were hardly out of my mouth when a rock we were passing some fifteen feet away suddenly rose out of the water and gazed at us with bulbous astonished eyes, snorting out two slender fountains of spray, like a miniature whale.

Fortunately, our gallant crew resisted the impulse to leap out of the canoe *en masse* and swim for the bank. The old man drew in his breath with a sharp hiss, and dug his paddle deep into the water, so that the canoe pulled up short in a swirl and clop of bubbles. Then we sat and stared at the hippo, and the hippo sat and stared at us. Of the two, the hippo seemed the more astonished. The chubby, pink-grey face floated on the surface of the water like a disembodied head at a séance. The great eyes stared at us with the innocent appraisal of a baby. The ears flicked back and forth, as if waving to us. The hippo sighed deeply and moved a few feet nearer, still looking at us with wide-eyed innocence. Then, suddenly, Agustine let out a shrill whoop that made us all jump and nearly upset the canoe. We shushed him furiously, while the hippo continued its scrutiny of us unabashed.

'No de fear,' said Agustine in a loud voice, 'na woman.'

He seized the paddle from the old man's reluctant grasp, and proceeded to beat on the water with the blade, sending up a shower of spray. The hippo opened its mouth in a gigantic yawn to display a length of tooth that had to be seen to be believed. Then, suddenly, and with apparently no muscular effort, the great head sank beneath the surface. There was a moment's pause, during which we were all convinced that the beast was ploughing through the water somewhere directly beneath us, then the head rose to the surface again, this time, to our relief, about twenty yards up-river. It snorted out two more jets of spray, waggled its ears seductively and sank again, only to reappear in a moment or so still farther upstream.

from *A Zoo in My Luggage* by Gerald Durrell

Thinking about the Writer's Technique

1 What scene does the writer present for the reader in the first paragraph?

2 How does the scene suddenly change?

3 Why does the writer compare the hippopotamus to a miniature whale?

4 What sound word does the writer use to indicate the old man drawing his breath?

5 What sound words does the writer use to describe the bubbles caused by the canoe stopping?

6 What was the hippo's face like?

7 What were the ears of the hippo doing?

8 What did the writer find amazing about the hippo's tooth?

9 How has the writer kept the reader's interest in this description of the encounter with a hippo?

10 Write down a sentence from this description which you particularly liked, then say why you have selected it.

WRITING ABOUT ANIMALS

Write two paragraphs about one of the following animals. In the first paragraph describe the animal's appearance. In the second paragraph describe its behaviour, habits or qualities.

- dog
- cat
- mouse
- lion
- rabbit
- emu
- kookaburra
- snake
- wasp

- elephant
- goat
- horse
- camel
- fox
- turkey
- magpie
- butterfly
- spider

- whale
- shark
- porpoise
- bear
- chicken
- sheep
- seagull
- mosquito
- rhinoceros

- kangaroo
- canary
- parrot
- eagle
- monkey
- seal
- panda
- duck
- pig

LANGUAGE

VERBS

Verbs express all kinds of actions. They are *doing, being* and *having* words. A verb can be just one word or it can be more than one word. Look at some of the verbs the author Robert C. O'Brien has used in *Mrs Frisby and the Rats of Nimh*. The verbs are shown in heavy type.

- The crow **was sitting** on the fence.
- She **thought** at first it **was** a hen.
- Mrs Frisby **walked** closer.

Identifying Verbs

Write down the following sentences taken from *Mrs Frisby and the Rats of Nimh* and underline the verbs. Some sentences have more than one verb.

1 She was startled by the sudden outburst of noise.

2 As she watched he fluttered to the top wire of the fence.

3 After a moment he spread his wings.

4 He was tied to the fence.

5 It looked like wire.

6 She thought of Timothy, and of the medicine she was carrying.

7 They were gliding to earth a yard from her front door.

8 She cut through the last strand, gave a tug, and the string fell off.

9 You saved my life.

10 I will remember.

Completing Sentences

Insert appropriate verbs of your own to complete these sentences.

1 An artist .... a picture.

2 A mechanic .... cars.

3 An author .... books.

4 A musician .... a musical instrument.

5 An apprentice .... a trade.

6 A detective .... crimes.

7 A geologist .... rocks.

8 A jockey .... horses.

9 A postman .... letters.

10 A soldier .... battles.

11 An archer .... arrows.

12 A barber .... hair.

13 A magician .... tricks.

14 A plumber .... water pipes.

15 A porter .... luggage.

VERBS TELL TIME

Verbs indicate the time an action takes place. There are three main time periods — *present*, *future* and *past*. This aspect of a verb is called its *tense*. For example:

Past tense: I ate
                 I have eaten
                 I had eaten
                 I was eating

Present tense: I eat
                 I am eating

Future tense: I will eat
                 I will be eating

Now look at the Garfield cartoon that follows. Identify the tense of the verbs in each picture.

Completing the Verb Table

Complete the following Verb Time Table.

Yesterday (past)	Today (present)	Tomorrow (future)
I awoke	I awake	I will awake
	I choose	
I began		
		I will catch
	I lose	
		I will pay
	I sell	
I knew		
		I will ring
	I fall	

Animal Verbs

Select verbs from the box and correctly insert them in the spaces below. The first one has been done to help you.

crows	purrs	gobbles	quacks
croaks	brays	hoots	roars
neighs	cheeps	buzzes	barks
laughs	coos	grunts	hisses

1 the rooster .crows...........   9 the frog ....

2 the duck ....   10 the chicken ....

3 the donkey ....   11 the bee ....

4 the horse ....   12 the dog ....

5 the cat ....   13 the snake ....

6 the owl ....   14 the kookaburra ....

7 the turkey ....   15 the dove ....

8 the lion ....   16 the pig ....

Verbs and Their Opposites

Write down the verbs listed in the left-hand column. Then match them up correctly with a verb opposite in meaning from the right-hand column.

grow	go
come	multiply
unite	wither
divide	advance
buy	fall
retreat	sell
remember	lengthen
harden	separate
import	hinder
rise	forget
shorten	export
help	soften

PUNCTUATION

THE COMMA

The comma is frequently used to mark a natural pause in a sentence — the place where a person would naturally take a breath before reading on.

Example: In a frenzy now that he had heard his mother, the baby fox moved about the cage, pulling at the wire and crying again and again.

Missing Commas

The following sentences are taken from *The Midnight Fox* passage. Write them down and insert the commas that are missing. Check the passage (pages 106–8) to see whether you have inserted the commas correctly.

1 I looked towards the garden because that's where the sound had come from but Uncle Fred did not even turn his head.

2 Just then there was the sound of thunder from the west a long rolling sound . . .

3 'Bless me is that thunder?'

4 We stood in the doorway feeling the breeze forgetting for a moment the baby fox.

5 I could not see any sign of the fox but I knew that she must be there.

6 The breeze quickened and abruptly the dishpan which Aunt Millie had left on the porch railing clattered to the floor.

7 It was a very final sound like the most important period in the world.

8 I went out the back door opening it so fast I hit the back of Uncle Fred's chair.

DRAMA

ACTING OUT FABLES

You can have much fun acting out fables. A fable is an animal story that teaches a lesson. The animal characters usually have the ability to speak and behave as humans do. Fables not only entertain us, but they also tell us important truths about human nature.

The most famous fables were those of a Greek slave named Aesop. Aesop was believed to have been living in Greece in the sixth century BC. Aesop invented wonderful stories about animals who spoke and acted as human beings did. His stories usually had a moral at the end.

Here are eight famous fables of Aesop. Arrange yourselves in pairs, then select one or two of the fables to act out in front of the class. Make sure one of the actors reads out the moral at the end of the fable.

The Crow and the Fox

A crow stole a large lump of cheese from a cottage windowsill and flew up to a high tree to eat it in comfort. A fox who was passing by noticed what she had in her beak and, his mouth watering at the sight, began to talk to her.

'O crow,' he said, 'what beautiful wings you have. How bright your eyes are. Your neck is as graceful as a swan's and your head looks as powerful as an eagle's.'

The crow wriggled and shifted on the branch with pleasure, fluffing out her feathers and trying to look fierce and noble.

'What a pity,' continued the fox, 'that a beautiful bird like you cannot speak. If only you could make a sound as beautiful as the colour of your feathers.'

This was too much for the crow. Determined to prove that her voice was as good as

her looks, she opened her beak and gave a loud 'caw'.

Down fell the cheese, right into the fox's open mouth.

'You may have a voice, crow, but you certainly haven't any brains,' he said as he walked away with the cheese.

Moral: *Vanity is expensive.*

The Lion and the Mouse

A mouse ran over the body of a sleeping lion. Waking up, the lion seized it and was minded to eat it. But when the mouse begged to be released, promising to repay him if he would spare it, he laughed and let it go. Not long afterwards its gratitude was the means of saving his life. Being captured by hunters, he was tied by a rope to a tree. The mouse heard his groans, and running to the spot freed him by gnawing through the rope. 'You laughed at me the other day,' it said, 'because you did not expect me to repay your kindness. Now you see that even mice are grateful.'

Moral: *Do not judge people's usefulness by their appearance.*

The Fox and the Sick Lion

An old lion, who was too weak to hunt or fight for his food, decided that he must get it by his wits. He lay down in a cave, pretending to be ill, and whenever any animals came to visit him, he seized them and ate them. When many had perished in this way, a fox who had seen through the trick came and stood at a distance from the cave, and inquired how he was. 'Bad,' the lion answered, and asked why he did not come in. 'I would have come in,' said the fox, 'but I saw a lot of tracks going in and none coming out.'

Moral: *Think for yourself. What everyone else is doing may not be the right thing.*

The Goose That Laid the Golden Eggs

A farmer and his wife once had a goose that laid a solid gold egg every day. Each evening they settled it securely in its pen in the corner of their kitchen with a bowl of the best corn and a saucer of fresh water. Each morning they found a new, bright yellow egg in its nest of sweet hay.

One day the farmer's wife said to her husband: 'These eggs are all very well, my dear, but though I suppose we will be rich in the end, it is a very slow way of making a fortune. By the time we get it, it will not be worth half what it is today. Now I have an idea. It is obvious to me that there must be a great store of golden eggs inside our goose. Why should we wait all our lives for her to lay them? Go and get the knife and we'll have all the gold now while we can still enjoy it.'

'Well,' said the farmer doubtfully, 'it seems a sad way to treat a good bird. But on the other hand . . .'

Without another word he killed the goose and cut her open — only to find that inside she was just like any other goose, with no sign of a golden egg at all.

'We'll not get rich quickly or slowly now, my dear,' said the farmer sadly.

Moral: *Don't be greedy.*

The Boy Who Cried Wolf

There was once a shepherd boy who looked after sheep for all the people in the village where he lived. Every morning he collected the sheep from their owners and drove them out onto the hills to feed. Every evening he rounded them carefully up and brought them home again.

Some days it was pleasant on the hillside and the time passed quickly. On other days the boy grew bored and restless with nothing to do but watch the sheep nibbling at the short grass from morning till night.

One day he decided to amuse himself.

'Wolf! Wolf!' he shouted at the top of his voice. 'A wolf is taking the sheep!'

The villagers all came rushing out of their houses to help him drive the wolf away — only to find the shepherd boy laughing till the tears rolled down his cheeks at the sight of their angry faces.

The boy tried the same trick again and again and each time the villagers rushed to his aid. Then, late one winter evening, just as the boy was thinking of gathering the sheep together to take them home, a real wolf came prowling around. The first the boy knew of it was a sound of frightened baaing from the sheep. Peering into the gloom he saw a long, grey shape creeping towards the flock.

The shepherd boy was very frightened. The wolf looked very big in the half darkness and he had only his crook to fight with.

Shouting 'Wolf! Wolf! A wolf is taking the sheep!' at the top of his voice, he raced towards the village. This time, however, the villagers did not come running out of their houses to fight the wolf. One or two of them looked up from what they were doing to grumble at the noise but most of them shrugged and said: 'He has played that trick once too often.'

Before the boy could find anyone to help him, the wolf had run off with all the sheep.

Moral: *No one believes a liar — even when he tells the truth.*

The Hare and the Tortoise

The hare was always laughing at the tortoise because he walked so slowly.

'Really I don't know why you bother to go at all,' she sneered. 'By the time you get there it will all be over — whatever it is.'

The tortoise laughed. 'I may be slow,' he said, 'but I bet I can get to the end of the field before you can. If you want to race, I'll prove it to you.'

Seeing an easy victory the hare agreed and she bounded off as fast as she could go. The tortoise plodded steadily after her.

Now it was the middle of a very hot sunny day and before long the hare began to feel a little drowsy.

'I think I'll just take a short nap under this hedge,' she said to herself. 'Even if the tortoise passes by I'll catch him up in a flash.'

The hare lay down in the shade and was soon fast asleep.

The tortoise plodded on under the midday sun.

Much later, the hare awoke. It was later than she had intended but she looked round confidently.

'No sign of old tortoise, I see, even if I did have rather more than forty winks.'

Away she went, running through the short grass and the growing corn, leaping ditches and brambles with ease. In a very short time she turned the last corner and paused for a moment to look at the place where the race was to end. There, not a yard from the finishing line was the tortoise, plodding steadily on, one foot after another, nearer and nearer to the end of the race.

With a great bound the hare streaked forward. It was too late. Though she threw herself panting over the line, the tortoise was there before her.

'Now do you believe me?' asked the tortoise. But the hare was too out of breath to reply.

Moral: *Slow and steady wins the race.*

The Travellers and the Bear

Two friends were travelling together when a bear suddenly appeared. One of them climbed up a tree in time and remained there hidden. The other, seeing that he would be caught in another moment, lay down on the ground and pretended to be dead. When the bear put its muzzle to him and smelt him all over, he held his breath — for it is said that a bear will not touch a corpse. After it had gone away, the other man came down from his tree and asked his friend what the bear had whispered in his ear. 'It told me,' he replied, 'not to travel in future with friends who do not stand by one in peril.'

Moral: *When you are in trouble you find out who your real friends are.*

The Fox and the Goat

A fox tumbled into a water tank and could not get out. Along came a thirsty goat, and seeing the fox asked him if the water was good. The fox jumped at the chance. He sang the praises of the water with all the eloquence at his command and urged the goat to come down. The goat was so thirsty that he went down without stopping to think and drank his fill. Then they began to consider how they were to get up again. 'I have a good idea,' said the fox, 'that is, if you are willing to do something to help us both. Be so kind as to place your forefeet against the wall and hold your horns straight up. Then I can nip up, and pull you up too.' The goat was glad enough to comply. The fox clambered nimbly over his haunches, shoulders, and horns, reached the edge of the tank, and began to make off. The goat complained that he had broken their compact. But he only came back to say: 'You have more hairs in your beard than brains in your head, my friend. Otherwise, you wouldn't have gone down without thinking how you were going to get up.'

Moral: *Look before you leap.*

THE NEWSPAPER

5

THE NEWSPAPER TODAY

WHAT'S IN THE NEWSPAPER?

Open any newspaper and you will be impressed by the amount of information that is presented to you. The first few pages are typically devoted to national and international news. This is followed by local news, feature articles, television and radio programme guides, reviews, comic strips and puzzles, the weather report, classified advertisements, the sport pages and much more. Photos and artwork of all kinds are used to create a newspaper that looks lively and interesting. In fact, most of the material contained in a newspaper can be summed up in two words: 'interest' and 'appeal'.

Nearly everything in a newspaper is designed to interest or appeal to someone. The reason for this is that a newspaper would soon fail to attract readers, and so fail to pay for its costs, if it did not offer a wide range of news, features and services.

One of the main functions of a newspaper is to acquaint its readers with the most important events and happenings of the day and to forecast their possible consequences. This is often called 'interpreting the news'.

THE FRONT PAGE

At the top of the front page is the newspaper's title, known as its 'masthead' or 'flag'. Near the masthead, which is often presented in ornate type, you will find the date of publication, the price of the paper and the paper's telephone number.

Here is a selection of newspaper mastheads. Notice how striking they are.

THE HEADLINES

When the newspaper boy or girl on the street corner yells *'Paper, paper, read all about it!'*, he or she often adds a few extra words such as *'Trains stop at midnight! Read all about it!'*. The headlines will probably persuade you to buy a paper — and to read all about it!

The most important headline in a newspaper is the one that runs across the top of the front page, under the masthead. This is called the 'banner headline'. On the following sample front page the banner headline is 'Just dropping into the office, dear'.

The West Australian

ESTABLISHED 1833   PERTH MONDAY AUGUST 1 1988   104 PAGES 50c*

Telephone 482 3111 (Classified 420 1111)

Just dropping into the office, dear

Becoming more and more tired of that ho-hum drive to work? Then meet a bunch of commuters with a difference... While most of Perth heads to their desks in the early-morning chill, 10 members of the Hillman Farm Skydiving Club prepare to parachute to the ground over Gloucester Park. The keen skydivers are jumping from a twin-engined Britten-Norman Islander and this spectacular picture is made possible by fellow sportsman and pilot Peter Wieland who manoeuvred his Cessna plane nearby. It's certainly a change from those daily traffic jams as the rest of us head for the city.

Picture: ROD TAYLOR

The purpose of a banner headline is to attract attention and sell newspapers. Look at the following headlines and note the methods used to attract the attention of potential readers.

Headlines	Methods Used to Attract Attention
KILLER BEES RAID PARKLANDS	This kind of headline is designed to shock people and so is called 'sensational'.
CYCLONE MOVES SOUTH	This headline presents a fact, but if you happen to live south of the cyclone you will, no doubt, buy a paper.
BOY CHASES LION	Such a headline suggests that a humorous story is to follow.
FLOOD CREEPS TOWARDS TOWN	Notice how the word 'creeps' gives the flood's progress a human quality, making it appear deliberate and somehow evil.
QUADS BREAK ALL RECORDS	This headline possesses strong human interest. People will ask themselves 'What records?' and buy a paper to find out.

Headline Exercise

Examine each headline and answer the question that accompanies it.

1 JUST DROPPING INTO THE OFFICE, DEAR

This headline, together with the photo of the parachutists jumping from the plane (opposite), would undoubtedly sell newspapers. Why?

2 TOWN'S 10 PM CURFEW FOR TEENS

This headline presents a fact. Why would such a fact be of interest to the general public?

3 WATER ON THE BRAIN CURED WITH TAP ON HEAD

Explain how this headline contains a humorous double meaning.

4 HUGE LOTTERY WIN FOR STRUGGLING FAMILY

In what way is strong human interest present in this headline?

5 WHIRLWIND LEAPS TOWN

How is the whirlwind made to seem human in this headline?

6 VIOLENCE. JUDGE HITS OUT

What do you think is the meaning of this headline?

7 FIRE DANGER WORSENS

How would readers react to this headline?

8 SHARK TERROR SHOCK

Explain why this headline can be called 'sensational'.

9 THE BIG MEN FLY

A dramatic photo is needed to illustrate this sports headline. Describe the kind of photo you would choose if you were the sports editor of the newspaper.

10 MAN RECOVERING AFTER FATAL CRASH

Explain what is wrong with this headline.

NEWS

Only the most important and interesting of the events and incidents that are occurring every day all over the world become news.

Below is a news item which was interesting enough to be circulated to newspapers everywhere. Read the news item carefully, then consider these important points of reporting.

1 The item consists of a photograph, a headline and five sections or paragraphs of description and comment.

2 Notice how the photograph has been angled to show the immense size of the man. This prepares us for the startling headline and story.

3 The first paragraph sets the scene for the unusual story that is to follow. What sad fact is revealed here?

4 The second paragraph tells us what was extraordinary about the removal of the overweight man from his bungalow. What extraordinary facts are presented in this paragraph?

5 The third paragraph carries the story a step further and also brings to light another strange fact about the man's existence. What is this strange fact?

6 The fourth paragraph gives us a glimpse of the man's past life. How is this done?

7 The final paragraph produces one more instance of the great difficulties of the man's life. What is this instance?

8 After you have read the news item, ask yourself whether you are satisfied with the way this news story has dealt with the overweight man's problems. If *you* were a reporter covering this story, what other aspects of this man's life might have interested you?

A 362-kilo headache

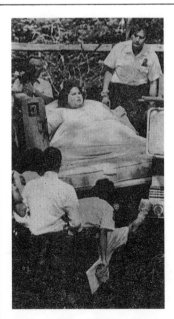

A 362-kilo (57 stone) man — too heavy to move himself from his specially built bed — was evicted from his dilapidated bungalow in Wesley Hills, New York, this week.

It was no ordinary eviction. A forklift was used to place Michael Edelman, 24, on a flat-bed lorry for a trip to hospital.

He will stay there until a flat is found that can be renovated to accommodate him. He cannot squeeze through an ordinary doorway.

Mr Edelman had lived in the bungalow for two years with his 170-kilo mother, Arlene.

He first came to public attention in December when he fell out of his bed and had to be lifted up by a tow truck.

Michael Edelman, still on his mattress, is placed on the back of a lorry.

THE 'GOOD NEWS' STORY

Amidst the usual bad news of disasters, famines and strife of all kinds, it is a relief for a newspaper reader to come across an obvious success story like the one shown opposite. Apart from its positive news value, the purpose of good news is to balance or offset the gloomy happenings that often dominate the news.

The first aspect of the article that attracts the reader is the photo with its strong human-interest appeal. The headline, too, promises some humour and also a story that is just a little out of the ordinary.

Scan the story for the source of its attraction as a 'good news' story, then answer the following questions.

Questions

1 Explain the pun (play on words) that occurs in the headline.

2 What is appealing about the photo?

3 How do the first two paragraphs of the story arouse our interest so that we want to read on?

4 Why is Penny's job both exciting and dangerous?

5 'Feeding time often becomes a brawling affair.' What does Penny mean by this?

6 Give the words in the story which link it to the photo.

7 What reasons does Penny give for *not* being afraid of sharks?

8 Why, according to Penny, do you 'still have to be careful'?

9 What is the biggest drawback of her job?

10 'You don't think about it usually, but sometimes . . . ' Why do you think the story ends with dots in this way?

11 In your opinion, what is the main appeal of this story?

Penny's work can have a real bite to it

by SHANE BURKE   Picture: PETER BARNES

When Penny Ajani packed her bags for Sydney two years ago she was looking forward to a job full of excitement.

But little did the Melbourne girl realise her job would involve swimming every day among some of the most feared killers of the deep.

Penny, 24, is one of 11 divers who take turns at hand-feeding a family of sharks in the world's largest sea aquarium — at Sydney's Darling Harbour.

Her charges include grey nurse, Port Jackson and carpet sharks and feeding time often becomes a brawling affair.

So it was a relief for Penny to be able to come eyeball to eyeball with a fish which was not the least interested in having a delectable diver for its next meal.

The former student, who turned professional diver three years ago, said sharks were not the man-eaters that people feared.

Friendly

Instead, the only Melbourne diver at the aquarium acclaimed by the Guinness Book of Records, said there was never a shortage of divers who wanted to feed the sharks.

Penny Ajani meets one of the smaller fry of the deep.

'Most sharks are probably more scared of people than people are of them,' she said yesterday.

'I love every minute of it down there . . . they're really quite friendly.

'But you still have to be careful because even though the sharks know the divers are there to feed them, they might decide they want a bit more.'

However, even this dare-devil diver admitted her job had its drawbacks.

No, it was not swimming alongside ravenous sharks, or having to help feed more than 5000 fish every day at the two-month old, $30 million aquarium.

'Cold water,' she said. 'You don't think about it usually, but sometimes . . .'

FEATURE ARTICLES

Apart from the daily news, there are interesting and well-developed articles and stories in newspapers which are called 'feature articles'. These typically deal with famous people, family life, personal experience, memories of childhood and many other topics. The style used may be humorous or serious.

The feature article shown opposite is by a well-known columnist, Mike Gibson. It deals with an aspect of the writer's boyhood, and is written in a style that is light and humorous.

Questions

1 Why is the title of this feature article a good one?

2 How is the reader's attention captured at the very start of the article?

3 Why do you think the subject of warts is likely to interest readers in general?

4 What was important about Dangerous Dan's missing wart?

5 What is the great mystery about warts?

6 What is the science fiction idea that is presented in the article?

7 What comparison does the writer use to indicate great size in a wart?

8 What are the two feelings the writer associates with being tackled at football and tearing off most of a wart?

9 Imagine a news item on warts. In what main ways do you think it would differ from Mike Gibson's feature article?

10 Did you like or dislike this feature article? Why?

MIKE GIBSON

The mysterious case of the disappearing wart

'It's gone!' he exclaimed, bounding in through the front door.

'What's gone?' I asked, thinking someone had knocked off my car, or maybe removed the front gate from its hinges.

'My wart,' he declared. 'Have a look, it's disappeared completely.'

And so it had. As our son Dangerous Dan presented his palm, like he wanted to borrow five bucks to go to the flicks with his mates, not a trace remained, not the slightest skerrick could be seen, of the rather large wart he had carried for years.

Our son, like his father before him, is no stranger to warts. We both carried them through childhood into our teenage years. But this was the symbolic one. This was the one that mattered. This was Dangerous Dan's last wart.

'So when did you realise it was gone?'

'I don't know,' he said, shaking his head. 'I was just sort of rubbing it this morning, and it wasn't there.'

Warts are like that. Particularly your last wart. For years, they sit there on your hand or your leg. For years you think you'll have them for the rest of your life. For years, you figure you'll never get a girlfriend because as soon as she sees your warts, she'll scream 'Blerk!' — and run for her life.

But then, one day, all of a sudden, they aren't there. One day, they are gone, and the way a wart disappears must be truly one of life's greatest and most enduring unsolved mysteries.

Forget about why, some summers, cicadas come out, while other summers they don't. Forget about why it always rains the day after you wash your car.

Sure, they're some of life's continuing mysteries, but they don't really compare to the enigma of how warts suddenly vanish.

Where do they go? Do they sort of melt overnight and get absorbed into your body? Do they fly off and spin around up there in the sky?

Who knows that way out there in the cosmos, countless billions of warts off countless billions of little boys' hands and legs, stockpiled since the birth of mankind, aren't breeding, ready to invade the planet Earth?

Who knows they haven't all stuck together to form one gigantic wart the size of the *Queen Mary*? When a wart like that falls out of the sky, hey, don't say I didn't warn you.

'You weren't playing with frogs last night, were you?' Dangerous Dan's mother chuckled.

'Frogs don't get rid of warts, frogs give them to you,' Dangerous Dan reminded her.

For all their wisdom, for all the things they know, warts are one thing mums aren't too clued-up about. Warts are men's business. No one has really experienced sheer panic and high anxiety, until they've torn off most of a wart when they get tackled playing football.

'I guess you won't miss your warts, Dan?' I asked.

'You bet I won't,' he replied.

And yet I wonder, when he grows up, when he becomes as old and silly as his dad, when he looks back on his youth that slipped away so fast, whether he won't look back and find a soft spot for that ever so rough spot.

A boys's last wart.

LETTERS TO THE EDITOR

The Letters to the Editor section of any newspaper provides readers with an opportunity to express opinions, offer comment and even give advice. Letters are sometimes written in response to an editorial, a news item or another reader's letter. Some letters raise personal concerns which are also of interest to other readers but which would not normally make the news. Editors tend to publish letters that present strong arguments either for or against an issue. The titles that introduce letters are chosen by the editor. Note that letter writers must give their names and addresses.

    Here are three letters to the editor. Notice that each letter expresses a strong point of view and that each issue raised is of concern to many of us.

Stop whingeing

I AM fed up reading about whingeing residents complaining about the noise created by garbage collectors.

    It would not matter what time these collections were made because someone would have a complaint. Do people want their garbage collected, or would they prefer to take it to the disposal dumps themselves?

    People are sleeping at all hours of the day and night. Someone has to be inconvenienced, or do the nine-to-fives think they are the only ones to be considered?

    Stop whingeing and be thankful someone is collecting your garbage.

Joan Barker,
Winmalee.

Questions

1 Why is the title 'Stop whingeing' likely to make you want to read the letter?

2 What feeling is being expressed by the writer as the letter begins?

3 What 'whingeing' is the writer referring to?

4 Why does somebody always have to be inconvenienced by garbage collection?

5 Why do you think the editor of the newspaper decided to publish this letter?

Captive condors

PETER Johnson's recent letter raised objections to the exhibition of Andean condors at the Adelaide Zoo.

Andean condors no longer 'soar blithely for miles, completely free'. They are highly prized for their meat and feathers and are shot at will by the local population.

The question of wild creatures confined for life does not consider the role zoos play in breeding and maintaining endangered species. The number of species, threatened by extinction in the wild, which have been saved by captive breeding in zoos is very great.

Captive animals and birds may be deprived of their freedom, to a certain degree, but, with many species of wildlife facing extinction, zoos may be the last hope.

**Gary Hawke,
Bridgewater.**

Questions

1 The first paragraph refers to a recent letter by Peter Johnson. What do you think his letter might have been about?

2 Condors are giant vultures whose habitat is the Andes. According to the letter writer, how do people like to think of condors in the wild?

3 What does the letter writer say is really happening to condors?

4 In what way could a zoo help to preserve an endangered species?

5 Captive animals and birds do suffer a loss in zoos. What is this loss?

Yes to dogs

FOR some time I have been seeking inspiration to find words in defence of our dogs, who seem to be fighting a losing battle in the discrimination stakes.

'No Dogs' here, 'No Dogs' there, the signs are increasing every day. Banning dogs, and consequently caring owners, is a popular bureaucratic hobby horse.

John Derum on 'That's Australia' gave me the answer. He told the story of a country hotel's reply to a man asking if he could bring his dog to the hotel, and it went something like this:
Dear Sir,

In 40 years of running this hotel I have never had to eject a dog for drunken behaviour; I have never found one of the hotel towels in a dog's suitcase; and I have never had the hotel bedclothes set on fire by a dog smoking in bed. Your dog will be welcome.

PS. If your dog can vouch for you, you can come too.

Gerry Cox,
Mooroolbark.

Questions

1 Explain why the title 'Yes to dogs' is likely to attract a reader's attention.

2 In your own words give the meaning of 'our dogs . . . seem to be fighting a losing battle in the discrimination stakes'?

3 What does the writer claim is happening 'every day'?

4 Who are banned along with the dogs?

5 What are the hotel owner's three reasons for *not* banning dogs from his hotel?

6 What is the surprise that is contained in the hotel owner's 'PS' to his letter?

7 Why do you think this letter would appeal to the editor of a large daily paper?

WRITING YOUR OWN LETTER TO THE EDITOR

Each member of the class is to produce a letter on one of the following topics. Volunteers should read letters to the class for comments and for votes on the most original letters.

1 Write a letter in reply to Joan Barker who is fed up with people whingeing about the noise made by garbage collectors. Adopt the position of someone who feels seriously affected by this noise in the early hours of the morning. Keep your letter as short as the original — or make it even shorter.

2 Write a letter which enthusiastically agrees or strongly disagrees with Gary Hawke's letter on zoos and captivity. Think of a creature other than the condor to illustrate the point or points you are making.

3 Write a strong letter which takes the view that dogs should be banned from most public areas. Produce reasons and examples to support your opinion.

4 Write a letter to the editor about any issue you feel should be raised.

NEWSPAPER CARTOONS

There are a number of cartoonists who are popular enough to be given considerable space in our daily newspapers. Their cartoons usually illustrate, in a striking way, items of news that have caught public attention.

Here the cartoonist is Zanetti. Consider the cartoon then answer the questions that follow.

Questions

1 Why do you think there is a newspaper with a headline in the bottom left corner of the cartoon?

2 What kind of TV news is being threatened with change?

3 The reader is left in no doubt that the setting for the cartoon is a TV studio. What part of the cartoon emphasises this setting?

4 How has the TV station changed the image of its news?

5 How has Zanetti achieved humour in this cartoon?

6 What is your own reaction to this cartoon?

7 Explain why violence in the news is a serious issue in our society.

NEWSPAPER ADVERTISEMENTS

Newspapers are popular for advertising commercial products. The more attractive and striking the advertisement, the more likely it is to reach the potential consumers of that product.

Most newspaper advertisements have three main purposes: the first is to attract attention, the second is to sustain interest and the third is to persuade the consumer to buy the product. Let's look at these three purposes in a little more detail. All successful advertisements must attract attention. Advertisers often achieve this by using a striking illustration or photograph. Once the reader's attention has been gained, the headline and the information about the product that follows must be interesting enough to sustain that attention. This may be possible if the product is shown to fill a need in a reader's lifestyle or business.

It is only a short step from having the need to own the product to having the desire to buy it. So, in the advertisement, there must be some way in which the reader can *act* on his or her desire to buy — a telephone number, a store to visit, or perhaps a cut-out coupon to send off. Sometimes a prompt response may mean a discount or even a gift!

Now let's look at a newspaper advertisement (opposite) that makes an impact.

Questions

1 Explain why this advertisement immediately attracts your attention.

2 The three words at the bottom of the photo are the Minolta 'motto'. Explain the meaning of each word.

3 Which of these three words is likely to give the most reassurance to a potential purchaser?

4 In what way is the headline (beginning 'The closest a photocopier . . .') related to the photo?

5 Read the first paragraph of the information. Why does the Minolta photocopier produce photocopies of 'such outstanding quality and clarity'?

6 Explain why the new 490Z photocopier is a world first.

7 How is the potential buyer reassured about after-sales support?

8 What need or desire in the reader does this advertisement appeal to?

9 If you were considering buying a photocopier, would this advertisement persuade you in favour of a Minolta? Why?

10 What is the link between Océ and Minolta?

11 How does this advertisement invite you to take action?

12 What do you think are the advantages and disadvantages of placing an advertisement in a newspaper rather than on TV or radio?

NEWSPAPER COMIC STRIPS

Sooner or later, most people who read a newspaper turn to the comic strips to follow the antics of their favourite characters, such as Hagar, Snoopy or the Wizard of Id.

Often the most popular comic strips are those that offer the reader a humorous insight into human nature or the problems of living in our modern world. The artist creates gestures, movements, facial expressions and balloons of speech that convey humorous messages to the readers.

Read and enjoy the typical newspaper comic strips that follow.

1 HAGAR THE HORRIBLE

Questions

1 In the first frame, what are the words in Hagar's greeting that offend Helga, his wife?

2 How would you describe the look on Hagar's face as he utters his greeting?

3 How does the artist indicate that the sound 'SPLAT!' is a wet one?

4 What has occurred in the third frame?

5 How has Hagar changed his greeting to satisfy Helga?

6 What problem or difficulty of modern living is highlighted in this comic strip?

2 THE WIZARD OF ID

Questions

1 How does the artist make the captured man look like a wrong-doer?

2 How would you describe the expression on the king's face in the first frame?

3 What change comes over the king's face in the third frame?

4 Why has the artist put the first letter of each word in the third frame in heavy black?

5 Why do you think this comic strip is funny?

3   BC

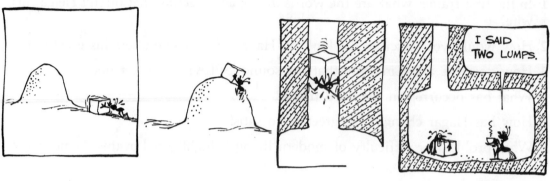

Questions

1 In the first frame, how does the artist show us that the ant is exerting a lot of energy?

2 What are the difficulties experienced by the ant in the second and third frames?

3 How is the extreme exhaustion of the ant that did all the work shown in the fourth frame?

4 What is the surprise that is revealed to the reader in the fourth frame?

5 Explain what is ridiculous about the lump of sugar and the cup of tea.

6 What does this comic strip say to us about the human feelings of gratitude and ingratitude?

4   PEANUTS

Questions

1 How does the artist indicate to the reader what Snoopy is typing?

2 How does the artist show that the girl is surprised and bewildered by what Snoopy is typing?

3 Do you think it is right or wrong of the girl to claim that because Snoopy is not beautiful he cannot write about beauty?

4 How does Snoopy react to her criticism?

5 Why do you think this comic strip would be popular with readers?

A NEWSPAPER CROSSWORD

Try solving this crossword about newspapers. Note that your clues refer to words that are all familiar ones in the newspaper world.

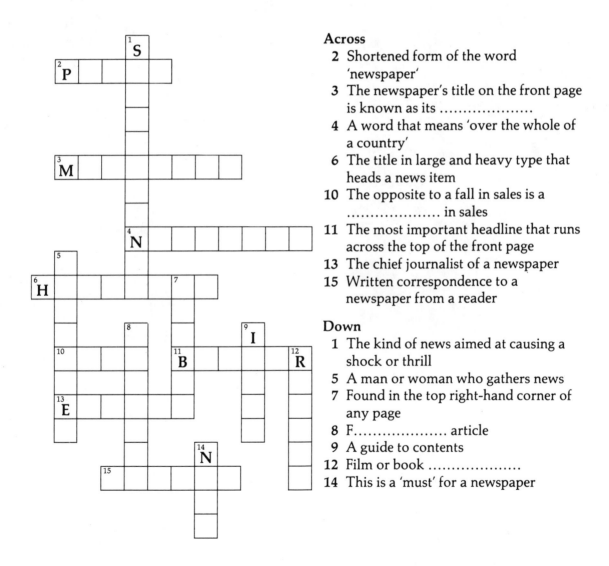

Across

2 Shortened form of the word 'newspaper'

3 The newspaper's title on the front page is known as its ....

4 A word that means 'over the whole of a country'

6 The title in large and heavy type that heads a news item

10 The opposite to a fall in sales is a .... in sales

11 The most important headline that runs across the top of the front page

13 The chief journalist of a newspaper

15 Written correspondence to a newspaper from a reader

Down

1 The kind of news aimed at causing a shock or thrill

5 A man or woman who gathers news

7 Found in the top right-hand corner of any page

8 F................... article

9 A guide to contents

12 Film or book ....

14 This is a 'must' for a newspaper

WAR

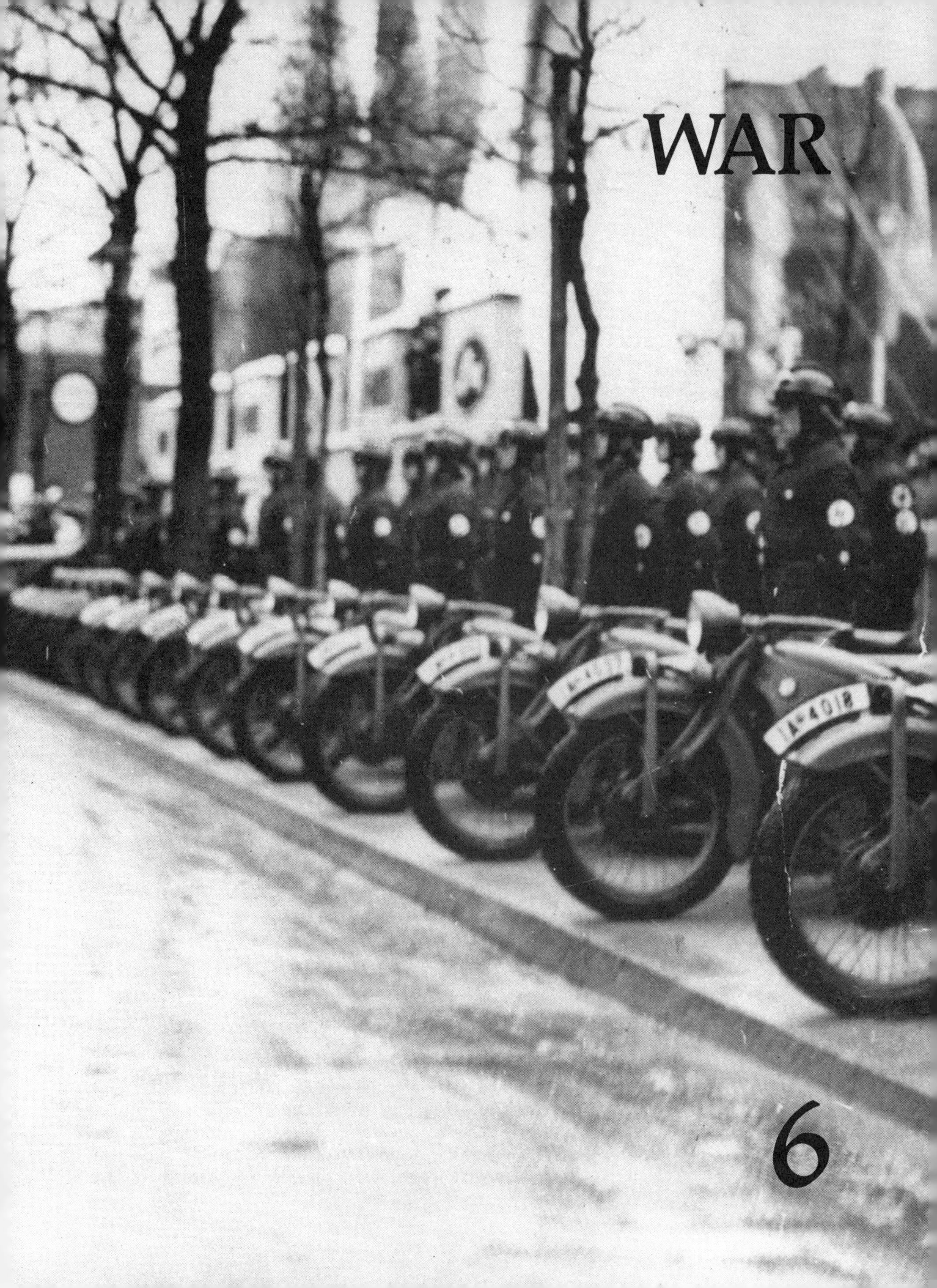

6

NOVELS

The Escape

I Am David is the story of a boy's struggle for survival as he tramps across Europe during the Second World War. In this extract, taken from the first few pages of the book, David is about to make his escape from a concentration camp.

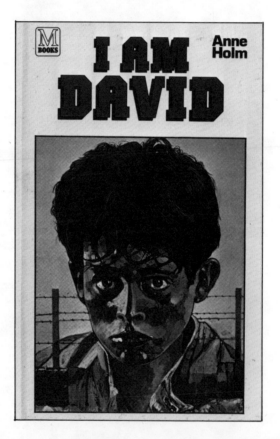

David was not yet sure whether he would make the attempt. He tried to work out why the man had told him to do it. It was certainly a trap: just as he was climbing over, the searchlight would suddenly swing round and catch him in its beam, and then they would shoot. Perhaps something pleasant was going to happen tomorrow and the man wanted him shot first. David had always known that the man hated him, just as much as David hated *him* in return. On the other hand, nothing pleasant had ever yet happened in the camp that David could remember, and he was now twelve years old — it said so on his identity card.

And then quite suddenly David decided he would do it. He had turned it over in his mind until his head was in a whirl and he still could not understand why the man had told him to escape. Suppose it were a trap and they shot him, it would all be over quickly anyway. If you were fired at while trying to escape, you would be dead within a minute. Yes, David decided to try.

There could not be many minutes left now. Over in the guard-room he could hear them moving about and getting dressed, and he could hear the guard yawning as his pace grew slower. Then came the sound of new steps and David pressed himself even more closely against the wall. It was the man; the faint sleepy yellow light from the guard-room shone for a moment on his face as he passed the window. He went up to the guard, and David suddenly felt quite empty inside and was sure that he would be unable to move when the time came. Then he saw before him the endless succession of days, months and years that would pass if he did not. The waiting would kill him in the end, but it might take years. And it would grow worse and worse, all the time: David clenched his teeth so hard that he felt the muscles of his throat grow taut. Then the man struck a match.

Nineteen, twenty . . . the half minute would be up when he had counted slowly to thirty . . . David set his foot in a gap higher up the barbed wire. . . . When would the searchlight come? They could not be certain of hitting him in the dark . . . and if they did not hurry he would be over.

A moment later he had touched the ground on the other side, and as he ran he said angrily to himself, 'What a fool you are! There's plenty of ground to cover yet — all this great flat stretch without so much as the stump of a tree for shelter. They'll wait till you've nearly reached the thicket . . . they'll think it more amusing if you believe you've almost got to safety.'

Why didn't they hurry up? The thought pounded through his head as every moment he expected to see the ground lit up in front of him. Then he stopped. He would run no more. When the beam of light caught him, they should see him walking away quite calmly. Then they would not enjoy it so much, they would feel cheated. The thought filled David with triumph.

When he was little, it had been his most burning desire to get the better of them, especially of the man. And now he would! They would be forced to shoot him as they watched him walking quietly away and taking no notice of them!

David was so taken up with his victory over them that he had gone a dozen yards past the spot where the thicket hid him from the camp before he realised that no one had fired. He stopped short. What could have happened? He turned, found a place where the thicket was thin enough to peer through and looked across at the low buildings outlined against the dark sky, like an even darker smudge of blackness. He could faintly hear the tread of the guard, but it came no nearer and sounded no different from usual, only farther off. Nothing at all appeared different.

David frowned in the darkness and stood for a moment undecided: it couldn't possibly . . .? He trotted on, following the edge of the thicket towards the big tree, running

faster the nearer he got, and when he reached the tree he threw himself down on the ground, searching frantically with his hands round the trunk.

There was the bundle. David leaned up against the tree shivering with cold although it was not cold at all. The bundle was a piece of cloth wrapped round something and tied in a knot. He fumbled with the knot, but his fingers were clumsy and would not respond — and then he suddenly realised that he dared not undo it. There would be something dangerous inside the bundle. . . . He tried to gather his thoughts together sufficiently to think what it might be, but his imagination did not get beyond a bomb.

It would make little difference, he thought desperately — a bullet or a bomb: it would soon be over, either way. Frantically, his fingers awkward, he struggled with the knot.

But there was no bomb in the cloth. It was a square handkerchief tied cross-wise over a bottle of water and a compass, just as the man had said. He barely managed to turn aside before he was sick.

Afterwards he felt carefully all round the square-shaped bundle. A bottle, a compass — there was something else. David's eyes had grown accustomed to the darkness: in the bundle there were also a box of matches, a large loaf of bread and a pocket-knife.

So the man had intended him to escape after all! A search-party would be sent out for him in the morning, but not before. The night was his, and it was up to him to make the most of it.

from *I Am David* by Anne Holm

Reading for Meaning

1 Why was David not sure that he would make his escape attempt?

2 How old was David? How did he know?

3 'Yes, David decided to try.' Why did David decide to make his escape attempt?

4 What did David think would happen to him while he was climbing over the barbed wire?

5 Why did David think they'd wait until he nearly reached the thicket before shooting at him?

6 What had been David's 'most burning desire' when he was little?

7 Why did it take David so long to realise that no one had fired?

8 'David leaned up against the tree shivering with cold although it was not cold at all.' Why do you think David was 'shivering'?

9 What did David think might be in the bundle? What was in the bundle?

10 'So the man had intended him to escape after all!' Why did David finally believe this?

11 What is the meaning of 'The night was his . . .'?

12 What does this passage tell you about David's character?

The Frozen Journey

When the Nazis occupied Poland at the beginning of the Second World War, three children — Ruth, Edek and Bronia — were separated from their parents. *The Silver Sword* describes their desperate attempt to find their parents again.

Others, laughing and making light of their experiences, told of miraculous escapes from the Nazis.

'I had a free ride on the roof of a Nazi lorry,' said one. 'It was eighty miles before I was seen. A sniper spotted me from the top of a railway bridge, but he couldn't shoot straight and I slid off into the bushes. The driver was so unnerved at the shooting that he drove slap into the bridge, and that was the end of him.'

Another told of a long journey on the roof of a train.

'I can beat that for a yarn,' said Edek.

Everyone turned round to look at the boy slumped down at the back of the truck. It was the first time he had spoken.

'I'll tell you if you'll give me a peep at the fire,' he said. 'And my sisters, too. And Jan. We're freezing out here.'

Ungrudgingly they made a way for the family — the only children in the truck — to squeeze through to the stove. Ruth carried Bronia, who did not wake, and she snuggled down beside it. Jan sat on the other side, with his chin on his knees and his arms clasping them. Edek stood up, with his back to the side of the truck. When someone opened the stove to throw in a log, a shower of sparks leapt up, and for a few moments the flames lit up his pale features.

'I was caught smuggling cheese into Warsaw, and they sent me back to Germany to slave on the land,' he said. 'The farm was near Guben and the slaves came from all parts of Europe, women mostly and boys of my age. In winter we cut peat to manure the soil. We were at it all day from dawn to dark. In spring we did the sowing — cabbage crop, mostly. At harvest time we packed the plump white cabbage heads in crates and sent them into town. We lived on the outer leaves — they tasted bitter. I tried to run away, but they always fetched me back. Last winter, when the war turned against the Nazis and the muddles began, I succeeded. I hid under a train, under a cattle wagon, and lay on top of the axle with my arms and legs stretched out.'

'When the train started, you fell off,' said Jan.

'Afterwards I sometimes wished I had,' said Edek, 'that is, until I found Ruth and Bronia again. Somehow I managed to cling on and I got a free ride back to Poland.'

Jan laughed scornfully. 'Why don't you travel that way here? It would leave the rest of us more room.'

'I could never do that again,' said Edek.

'No,' said Jan, and looked with contempt at Edek's thin arms and bony wrists. 'You're making it all up. There's no room to lie under a truck. Nothing to hold on to.'

Edek seized him by the ear and pulled him to his feet. 'Have you ever looked under a truck?' he said, and he described the underside in such convincing detail that nobody but Jan would have questioned his accuracy. The boys were coming to blows, when the printer pulled Jan to the floor and there were cries of, 'Let him get on with his story!'

'You would have been shaken off,' Jan shouted above the din, 'like a rotten plum!'

'That's what anyone would expect,' Edek shouted back. 'But if you'll shut up and listen, I'll tell you why I wasn't.' When the noise had died down, he went on. 'Lying on my stomach, I found the view rather monotonous. It made me dizzy too. I had to shut my eyes. And the bumping! Compared with that, the boards of this truck are like a feather bed. Then the train ran through a

puddle. More than a puddle — it must have been a flood, for I was splashed and soaked right through. But that water saved me. After that I couldn't let go, even if I'd wanted to.'

'Why not?' said Jan, impressed.

'The water froze on me. It made an icicle of me. When at last the train drew into a station, I was encased in ice from head to foot. I could hear Polish voices on the platform. I knew we must have crossed the frontier. My voice was the only part of me that wasn't frozen, so I shouted. The station-master came and chopped me down with an axe. He wrapped me in blankets and carried me to the boiler-house to thaw out. Took me hours to thaw out.'

'You don't look properly thawed out yet,' said the printer, and he threw him a crust of bread.

Other voices joined in. 'Give him a blanket.' 'A tall story, but he's earned a bed by the stove.' 'Another story, somebody! One to make us forget.' 'Put some romance in it.'

The stories petered out after a while. When it was quiet, and the refugees, packed like sardines on the floor of the truck, lay sleeping under the cold stars, Ruth whispered to Edek, 'Was it really true?'

'Yes, it was true,' said Edek.

'Nothing like that must ever happen to you again,' said Ruth.

from *The Silver Sword* by Ian Serraillier

Reading for Meaning

1 What did the person on the roof of the lorry do when the German sniper started shooting at him?

2 What happened to the German lorry? Why?

3 Why were the children allowed to come close to the fire?

4 What happened to Edek when he was caught smuggling cheese into Warsaw?

5 What kind of work did Edek do on the farm?

6 In what way was life hard on the farm?

7 How did Edek travel under the train?

8 What reasons does Jan give for not believing that Edek travelled underneath a train carriage?

9 Why were the boys 'coming to blows'?

10 What did Edek do to overcome his dizziness when he was lying under the railway truck?

11 Why did the water save Edek?

12 How did Edek know he had crossed the frontier?

13 How did the station-master remove Edek from under the train?

14 How do you know that Ruth is sympathetic towards Edek?

15 What did you learn about Edek's character from this incident?

Fear

Lee and his family decide to escape from Vietnam with forty people crammed tightly in a rickety boat. Here is the refugees' encounter with a hostile patrol boat.

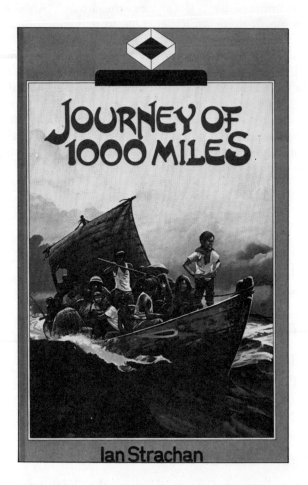

JOURNEY OF 1000 MILES

Ian Strachan

'Get down, everybody!'
Lee looked up and saw, some distance off but coming towards them, red and green navigation lights and knew it must be a naval patrol boat because of its speed.

As the deep-throated thrum of the boat's powerful engines drew closer Lee crouched down still retching and lay huddled in a miserable heap surrounded by the smell of his own bile.

Kim let out a startled cry as the brilliant beam of a searchlight pierced the darkness and swept the fishing boat from stem to stern. By its reflected light Lee could clearly see the haunted look on the faces of the other passengers. It was a sharp contrast to the almost holiday atmosphere which had begun to develop on the boat as it got into the estuary when everybody was busy settling in and introducing themselves.

Lee knew that if the patrol boat got close enough, its men would be bound to see the people crouched down in the fishing boat. Surrounded by the smell of fish, tar, engine oil and vomit he began to feel hot and dizzy. His body was stiff with fear, aching from seasickness and he felt he might faint at any moment. To keep himself conscious he twisted his neck round so that he could see Trinh standing in the stern holding the tiller. He was blinking in the harsh light but he managed to wave back at the patrol boat as if he hadn't a care in the world.

A Tannoy was switched on aboard the patrol boat and a voice, made harsh and thin by its horn, demanded, 'Where are you bound?'

Trinh shrugged and shouted back. 'Tell me where the fish run and I'll tell you where I'm bound.'

The noise of the patrol boat's idling engines drowned his voice.

'Say again!' barked the hailer.

'Anywhere where there's fish,' Trinh shouted back.

There was a pause. The boats drifted closer to each other.

'Why aren't you showing navigation lights?'

Lee watched as Trinh pretended to look puzzled and leant out over the side as if to see what they said were true.'They must have blown out,' he apologised with a shrug. 'I'll light them again as soon as you stop rocking me about like this.'

There was another, longer pause. The boats kept drifting closer and Lee, not daring to breathe again, watched as the spotlight dipped and bobbed with the motion of the patrol boat, convinced it would only be seconds before a sailor on its bridge got a glimpse of somebody's back.

Aboard the patrol boat, the captain was wondering if if would be worthwhile searching this dowdy old fishing boat for contraband when the radio crackled into life.

Abruptly, without another word being exchanged, the light snapped off and the patrol boat revved its engines speeding off into the dark, leaving the fishing boat bobbing about like a cork in its vicious wake.

In the darkness which followed the spotlight's glare the passengers began to relax.

'What happened — why did they go away?' Lee asked.

'Perhaps they were called away to something more important,' father suggested.

'But they will have noted the identity number of this boat,' grandfather said quietly. 'Whatever happens we'll *have* to keep going now.'

Lee clutched his sore stomach. He wondered if the prospect of weeks at sea was quite the adventure he'd expected.

from *Journey of 1000 Miles* by Ian Strachan

Reading for Meaning

1 How did Lee know that the boat coming towards them must be a naval patrol boat?

2 Why did Kim let out a startled cry?

3 How did the other people react to the searchlight?

4 What did Lee think men on the patrol boat would see if the patrol boat got too close?

5 How was Lee feeling?

6 What did Trinh manage to do while the searchlight was on him?

7 What information did the patrol boat want from Trinh?

8 What does Trinh say to give the impression to the patrol boat that his boat is a fishing vessel?

9 What excuse does Trinh give for not showing navigational lights?

10 '. . . Lee, not daring to breathe again . . .' Why was Lee so worried?

11 What prevented the patrol boat captain from searching the fishing boat for contraband?

12 What caused the fishing boat to be 'bobbing about like a cork'?

13 Why, according to Lee's father, did the patrol boat go away?

14 What comments would you make about Trinh's character?

15 Did you enjoy reading this story? Why or why not?

POETRY

POEMS OF WAR

Uncle Bert

My one-armed uncle Bert
Married a girl from Aberaman
And rented a tiny cottage in a dingle
At the end of a cart-track
Above the village of Brockweir.
There he toiled, earned a living
And raised six children.

He made fences, gates and cots,
Tended a kitchen garden,
Learnt all about animals
And became a countryman.
He did all this with a sleeve
Half empty and a right arm
As strong as a stout oak-branch.

In his youth he played the violin
With skill and lived at Gilfach.
At eighteen he was at Dardanelles
To maintain England's Glory.
But he never reached land
For as he waded in the sea
A Turk shot off half his arm.

For two years his violin
Hung above his soldier photograph.
My grandmother, his mother, told me
That on his return, his sleeve
Pinned to his shoulder,
He took down his instrument
And smashed it on the garden wall.

Robert Morgan

Questions

1 Why is the poet's uncle Bert different from other people?

2 'He made fences, gates and cots'. What does this show about Bert?

3 What is the meaning of '. . . with a sleeve/Half empty'? What other words later in the poem repeat this idea?

4 What does the poet reveal to the reader about Bert's right arm?

5 What does the poet tell you about Bert's youth?

6 What happened to Bert as he was coming ashore at Dardanelles?

7 Where was Bert's violin when he was away at the war?

8 'He took down his instrument/And smashed it on the garden wall'. Why do you think Bert did this?

9 What does this poem show you about war?

10 What are your feelings towards Bert?

11 Why do you think the poet wrote this poem?

12 Did you enjoy reading this poem? Why or why not?

If I Die in War

If I die in War
You remember me;
If I live in Peace
You don't.

Spike Milligan

TV News

I sat and ate my tea
And watched them die
And knew at twelve
That brave men died
On either side.
And that is why
At twelve I cried — and cried,
And couldn't understand
My father's beaming pride.

John Kitching

The Boat People's Prayer for Land

Lost in the tempests
Out on the open seas
Our small boats drift.
We seek for land
During endless days and endless nights.
We are the foam
Floating on the vast ocean.
We are the dust
Wandering in endless space.
Our cries are lost
In the howling wind.
Without food, without water
Our children lie exhausted
Until they cry no more.
We thirst for land
But are turned back from every shore.
Our distress signals rise and rise again
But the passing ships do not stop.
How many boats have perished?
How many families lie beneath the waves?
Lord Jesus, do you hear the prayer of our flesh?
Lord Buddha, do you hear our voice
From the abyss of death?
O solid shore,
We long for you!
We pray for mankind to be present today!
We pray for land to stretch its arms to us!
We pray that hope be given us
Today, from any land.

A poem written by an unknown Vietnamese at a refugee camp in 1978

Questions

1 'Lost in the tempests'. What is happening to the boat people?

2 Why are the days and nights 'endless' for the boat people?

3 Why does the poet refer to the boat people as 'foam'?

4 Why does the poet refer to the boat people as 'dust'?

5 What suffering do the children of the boat people experience?

6 What is the meaning of 'We thirst for land'?

7 What happens to the boat people when they land in other countries?

8 How do the passing ships react to the boat people's distress signals?

9 What do the boat people pray for in the last four lines of the poem?

10 After reading this poem, what are your feelings towards the boat people?

The Long Flight

'. . . a German Dornier bomber crashed into a ploughed field in North Wales and lay undetected for 43 years. The plane, with its bomb load intact, was shot down on its way to Liverpool on October 16, 1940 and buried itself in the soft ground, killing all the crew.' (The Guardian 28.9.83)

From darkening Cherbourg airfield they took off
At twenty hundred hours, young crews but tough
And hardened to their work, a bomber squadron
Of Dornier Seventeens. They headed on
Towards the English Channel, their target Liverpool.
Hard to spot against the smeared autumnal
Skies they looked, from earth, like iron crosses
Or, black against pale lunar breast, like brooches,
Bird-shaped, sliding into folds of dark.
And soon, above the Wessex coast, the crack
And thud of anti-aircraft guns hurled up
Their brilliancies of rage, the probe and dip
Of searchlights swung like white sticks of the blind.
One plane was hit. It lurched and bucked, then climbed
But fiery pennants flew from starboard wing
Until the wind's rush ripped them off and flung
Them down to the floor of night. The plane went on
Though engine-cough said damage had been done
And slowly altitude and speed decreased
Till they had lost all contact with the rest.
And so, alone, the broken aircraft droned
Low over Denbigh Moor then turned for home.
Too late. Its single engine faltered, cut:
The pilot snarled and sweated as he fought
To bring back power. The crew was clenched and white,
Silent as the drowned. The plane's nose dipped
And through the wind's black howl they plummeted
To where ploughed earth was goffered like the sea
And like the sea earth hungered for the crew.

The plane went down; it sank in troughs of soil,
Down into darkness, deep in loam and marl,
Silent, dark as ocean's shifting gloom.
Then spectral engines purred again: they flew,
Flew blind with shattered instruments for more
Than forty years in fossil silence, war,
With never hope of armistice. Now gulls
And curlews wheel and cry above, their calls
Bleak requiem for what they see down there —
The shadowed shape, the giant bird entombed,
Wings cruciform as if it rode the air.

Vernon Scannell

Questions

1 How do you know that night was falling as the planes were taking off?

2 What kind of men made up the bomber crews?

3 What was the destination of the German bombers?

4 What did the bombers look like up in the sky?

5 What sounds did the anti-aircraft guns make?

6 What happened to the plane immediately after it was hit?

7 What is the meaning of 'engine cough'?

8 'Till they had lost all contact with the rest'. Why did they lose contact?

9 Why does the poet refer to the plane as 'the broken aircraft'?

10 How did the pilot react to the single engine cutting out?

11 Why do you think the crew was 'clenched and white'?

12 '. . . they plummeted/To where ploughed earth was goffered like the sea'. What has happened to the plane?

13 What picture do you see in the words 'the giant bird entombed'?

14 Why do you think the poet called his poem 'The Long Flight'?

15 What were your feelings towards the men in the plane?

WRITING

SCRIPTWRITING

Scriptwriters play an important, unseen role in today's society. For every play, film and television series that you watch, there must be scripts for the actors to work from. Quite often films and television dramas are developed from novels or short stories. When this happens, the film producer will have previously purchased the film or television rights of a book. Then a scriptwriter or a team of scriptwriters will have been employed to convert the book into a script.

Now read through the passage 'The Hiding Place' which has been taken from the novel *The Silver Sword*. Then read the script that Stuart Henson has developed from this passage. As the scene begins, Joseph Balicki, a former headmaster of a Polish school, has just managed to escape from a Nazi prison camp. Dressed in a stolen German soldier's uniform, he is seeking refuge from his pursuers.

The Hiding Place — Novel

A wood fire was burning in a wide open hearth. A large pot hung above it from a hook in the chimney. An old lady was sitting by the fire. She looked startled.

Joseph threw his cap and greatcoat over a chair.

'Here's the pistol I almost shot you with,' he said. 'It's a slab of chocolate.'

He broke it into three pieces, giving one to each of them. They were suspicious and waited till Joseph had swallowed his piece before they ate theirs.

'I don't understand,' said the peasant slowly. 'You speak like a Pole. You look like a Pole. But your uniform —'

At that moment a bell clanged out from the other side of the valley. It echoed among the mountains.

'That's the prison bell,' said Joseph. 'It's a long time since it rang like that — when the last prisoner escaped.'

'You've come to search for him?' asked the old lady.

'I am the prisoner,' said Joseph. 'I knocked out a guard and stole his uniform. Look — if you don't believe me, here's my camp number burnt into my arm — ZAK 2473. I want you to hide me.'

The number convinced them that he was telling the truth. They knew that if they were found hiding him they would die. But they were brave people and did not hesitate.

Joseph slept in a warm bed that night for the first time for two years.

In the morning the old man went to work the luggage lift as usual. Before going, he arranged a danger signal. If there were any soldiers coming across in the cage, he would whistle three times. And he showed Joseph a hiding place in the woodshed.

While he was away, Joseph showed the old woman the tattered photos of his family. He had taken them out of his wallet so many times to look at them that they were creased and crumpled and finger-marked all over. He spoke about his wife and children, his school, his capture by the Nazis; about the shortage of food, the destruction everywhere, and the continual fear of arrest. Every day had brought news of more families being split up.

from *The Silver Sword* by Ian Serraillier

The Hiding Place — Script

Joseph   *(More gently)*   Do as I tell you and you'll come to no harm. Do you live here? *(Peasant nods)*   Take me inside!

(Lights up on peasant croft interior: two boxes for seats by hearth. Peasant's wife is polishing a pot.)

Joseph   *(Throwing greatcoat over a box)*   Here's the pistol I almost shot you with! It's a slab of chocolate.   *(He breaks it into three. Peasants wait suspiciously until he eats before swallowing theirs.)*

Peasant   I don't understand. You look like a Pole. You speak like a Pole. But your uniform. . . .   *(Sound of bell, distant.)*

Joseph   That's the prison bell. It's a long time since it rang like that — when the last prisoner escaped.

Wife   You've come to search for him?

Joseph   I am the prisoner. I knocked out the guard and stole his uniform. Look if you don't believe me, here's my convict's number burnt into my arm.   *(Pause)*   I want you to hide me!

(Peasant and Wife turn heads to one another, freeze.)

Edek   *(Narrator)*   That night Joseph slept in a warm bed for the first time in two years. In the morning the old man went to work as usual. They arranged a danger signal. They knew if they were found hiding him they would die, but they were brave people and did not hesitate.

(Edek turns towards peasant croft interior. Joseph in shirt sleeves, washing in bowl.)

Peasant   Very good! I must go now. If there are soldiers coming across in the mountain lift I shall whistle, three times   *(Demonstrates)*   OK?

Joseph   *(Drying on towel)*   Thank you!

Peasant   You will have time to get to the woodshed. The hiding place is well concealed. My wife will stack timber over the entrance. They will not find you there. *(Wife nods)*   Goodbye my friend!

Joseph   Goodbye — and thank you again.

Peasant   We would do the same always. Every prisoner is someone's son.   *(Exit)*

Wife   Our own son — he is your age — he was fighting in Kalisz. We have not heard from him for seven months.

(Joseph looks at the peasant woman. Sympathy and sorrow move him to speak but he can say nothing. Seeing it has struck a sombre note, the Wife changes the subject, bustling to the window with the bowl, folding the towel.)

Wife   You have children of your own? It is a long time too since you have seen them?

Joseph   *(Sits slowly, takes wallet and photos from greatcoat pocket)*   Yes, Mother, I have three children. They were in Warsaw. I do not know what has become of them.

Wife   *(Crosses to stand behind Joseph)*   Oh, they're fine upright children. The smallest, she's so pretty! What is she called.

Joseph   That is my Bronia. This is Ruth. Edek is the middle one. He is very serious, very determined. You can see he does not smile very often, but when he does . . . This is my wife. See how Ruth is like her. Ruth will be a teacher one day — a great teacher I think. Not like me. I am not a learned man. I work in the primary school in the East Side of the city. At least, I *did* work. I was taken by the Secret Police. We read our lessons in Polish.

Wife   I understand.

Joseph   *(Looks down at the photo again)*   Ruth reads all the time. Everything. Anything. She is a true scholar. But this war . . .
There is no food in Warsaw. Everyone is afraid. You can see fear hiding in people's eyes. Sometimes I think you can even *smell* fear. It's like a fog. People no longer live their own lives. There are few families that have stayed together now in Warsaw.

from *The Play of the Silver Sword* by Stuart Henson

WRITING YOUR OWN SCRIPTS

As you read through the script of 'The Hiding Place', you would have noticed that it is set out very differently from the passage in the novel. The script is written so that it can be performed on stage. The characters' names appear prominently before each speech and stage directions are given in italics to help the actors.

This next passage from *The Silver Sword* follows on from the one you have just read. Read it through carefully. Your task is to turn it into a script so that it can be performed for the class.

A Lucky Escape

The old woman was moved by his story. While he was speaking, she began to think of ways in which she could help him. He looked starved and needed good food. She had a little cheese and oatcakes, a side of bacon hanging in the cellar, and the remains of a tin of real coffee saved from before the war.

Suddenly there was a loud bang on the door. Was it a search party? If so, why had the old man given no warning?

A voice called out in German.

There was no time to escape to the wood-shed.

'Quick — up there!' The old woman pointed up the chimney. 'There's an opening on the right, half-way up.'

Joseph dived into the hearth and hauled himself up over the iron spit. The fire was only smouldering and there was not much smoke. He had not found the opening when the door burst open and two soldiers came in. While they searched the room, he stood very still, his legs astride the chimney. He wanted to cough. He thought his lungs would burst.

Suddenly a head peered up the chimney. It was the old woman. 'They've gone upstairs,' she said. 'But don't come down yet.'

She showed him where the opening was. He crept inside, coughing. He could see the sky through the chimney top above him.

He was congratulating himself on his good luck when he heard the soldiers return to the room below. With difficulty he controlled his cough.

'What about the chimney?' said the other soldier. 'Your uniform's older than mine. What about you going up?'

'Not likely.'

'Then we'll send a couple of bullets up for luck.'

Two ear-splitting explosions. It seemed as if the whole chalet was falling down. Joseph clung on to his perch. There was a great tumbling about his ears. He clung and clung and clung — till his fingers were torn from their grip, and he fell.

When he came to his senses, he was lying on the floor. The old woman was bending over him, washing his face with cold water.

'It's all right — they've gone,' she said. 'The fall of soot saved you. The soldiers ran for it when the soot came down. They were afraid for their uniforms.'

'I'm sorry I didn't have time to warn you,' said the old man. 'The soldiers had hidden themselves in the cage. I didn't see them till it was too late.'

from *The Silver Sword* by Ian Serraillier

You can have fun changing the following passage from the novel *The Twits* into a short script. The action revolves around only two characters, Mr and Mrs Twit, so your task will be a fairly simple one.

The Glass Eye

And then there was the glass eye. Mrs Twit had a glass eye that was always looking the other way.

You can play a lot of tricks with a glass eye because you can take it out and pop it back in again any time you like. You can bet your life Mrs Twit knew all the tricks.

One morning she took out her glass eye and dropped it into Mr Twit's mug of beer when he wasn't looking.

Mr Twit sat there drinking the beer slowly. The froth made a white ring on the hairs around his mouth. He wiped the white froth on to his sleeve and wiped his sleeve on his trousers.

'You're plotting something,' Mrs Twit said, keeping her back turned so he wouldn't see that she had taken out her glass eye. 'Whenever you go all quiet like that I know very well you're plotting something.'

Mrs Twit was right. Mr Twit was plotting away like mad. He was trying to think up a really nasty trick he could play on his wife that day.

'You'd better be careful,' Mrs Twit said, 'because when I see you starting to plot, I watch you like a wombat.'

'Oh, do shut up, you old hag,' Mr Twit said. He went on drinking his beer, and his evil mind kept working away on the latest horrid trick he was going to play on the old woman.

Suddenly, as Mr Twit tipped the last drop of beer down his throat, he caught sight of Mrs Twit's awful glass eye staring up at him from the bottom of the mug. It made him jump.

'I told you I was watching you,' cackled Mrs Twit. 'I've got eyes everywhere so you'd better be careful.'

from *The Twits* by Roald Dahl

GROUP SCRIPTWRITING

Divide into small groups. Then select a passage from your class novel that you think could be changed into an interesting script. Using the same techniques that you observed being used by the scriptwriter Stuart Henson in *The Play of The Silver Sword*, convert your passage into a script. Once this has been done, you should make multiple copies of your script and have members of your group act out the scene for the class.

LANGUAGE

MORE ON VERBS

Verbs in Action

Read the poem 'Thunder and Lightning'. Observe how the verbs give life and action to the thunder and lightning. Write out the poem and underline the verbs.

Thunder and Lightning

Blood punches through every vein
As lightning strips the windowpane

Under its flashing whip, a white
Village leaps to light.

On tubs of thunder, fists of rain
Slog it out of sight again.

Blood punches the heart with fright
As rain belts the village night.

James Kirkup

Write down these proverbs and underline the verbs. Some of the proverbs have more than one verb.

1 Look before you leap.

2 The early bird catches the worm.

3 Every cloud has a silver lining.

4 When the cat is away, the mice will play.

5 A drowning man clutches at a straw.

6 People who live in glass houses should not throw stones.

7 Strike while the iron is hot.

8 Rome was not built in a day.

9 Make hay while the sun shines.

10 A fool and his money are soon parted.

Everyday Verbs

In the box are verbs that are used in everyday life. Correctly insert the verbs from the box in the spaces below.

rehearse	invest	inflate	narrate
inhale	exterminate	navigate	accelerate
irrigate	light	quench	shrug
lubricate	celebrate	shuffle	shut

1 .... a fire	9 .... a birthday
2 .... a play	10 .... smoke
3 .... money	11 .... pests
4 .... a story	12 .... dry land
5 .... a ship	13 .... your feet
6 .... machinery	14 .... your eyes
7 .... a tyre	15 .... your thirst
8 .... your speed	16 .... your shoulders

Sound Verbs

Some verbs suggest the actual sound of the action they represent. Match each noun in the left-hand column with a suitable sound verb from the right-hand column.

Nouns	Sound Verbs
coins	screech
raindrops	pops
a fire	chimes
brakes	jingle
a clock	bubbles
a telephone	drips
a tap	patter
a cork	crackles
a brook	rings

Using Correct Verb Forms

Write down the following sentences and insert in the spaces the correct verb forms from within the brackets. The first one has been done for you.

1a The surfer ...swam......... through the breakers.
b The surfer had ...swum......... through the breakers.   (swum/swam)

2a The traveller was .... to England.
b The pilot .... to England.   (flown/flew)

3a The tiler has .... from the roof.
b The tiler .... from the roof.   (fallen/fell)

4a The gaoler .... the prisoner some food.
b The prisoner was .... food by the gaoler.   (given/gave)

5a The author .... a letter to his editor.
b The author has .... a letter to his editor.   (wrote/written)

6a The cartoonist .... a comic picture.
b A comic picture had been .... by the cartoonist.   (drawn/drew)

7a The deputy principal .... the culprit.
b The culprit was .... to the deputy principal.   (knew/known)

8a The student .... her apple.
b The apple had been .... by the student.   (ate/eaten)

9a She .... the car through the city.
b The car was .... at a high speed.   (driven/drove)

10a She .... to visit Ireland.
b She has .... to visit Ireland.   (chose/chosen)

Verbs with Similar Meanings

Match up each verb from the left-hand column with the verb having a similar meaning from the right-hand column.

demonstrate	dig
cease	hide
protect	stop
see	hate
abandon	waste
conceal	leave
detest	expect
anticipate	guard
excavate	show
squander	perceive

PUNCTUATION
MORE USES OF THE COMMA

- Commas are used to separate a number of adjectives describing a person. (Generally the comma is not inserted before the 'and'.)

  Example: David was bold, steadfast, determined and decisive.

- Commas are used to separate items in a list.

  Example: The camper carried a rope, a blanket, a haversack and a small tent.

- A comma is used to separate the name of the person spoken to, or addressed, from the rest of the sentence.

  Example: 'Tell us a story, Edek.'

- A pair of commas is often used to separate a phrase from the rest of the sentence.

  Example: London, the capital of England, is a very old city.

Adding Commas

Write out the following sentences and correctly insert the missing commas.

1 Ruth Jan Bronia and Edek were allowed to approach the fire.
2 The captives came from Poland Holland Belgium and Czechoslovakia.
3 Berlin a large city in Germany was bombed during World War II.
4 'Steer the ship Trinh.'
5 David a boy of great courage managed to gain his freedom.
6 Lee was surrounded by the smell of fish tar engine oil and sickness.
7 A voice harsh and thin came from the patrol boat.
8 Kim Trinh and Lee were boat people.
9 David shivering with the cold was leaning against the tree.
10 The bundle contained a bottle a compass a pocket-knife a box of matches and a large loaf of bread.

DRAMA

The Play of The Silver Sword

by Stuart Henson
(from the novel by Ian Serraillier)

Ruth, Edek and Bronia have escaped from the Nazis and have found a home in the cellar of a bombed house. The narrator, Joseph, is the children's father. Now act out the scenes that follow.

CHARACTERS

Bronia	Soldier 1
Ruth	Soldier 2
Edek	Eva
Joseph	Jan
Peasant	Kate

SCENE 1

The cellar. Ruth and Bronia set up box furniture. Ruth sits and begins to match two tatty ends of curtain. Bronia is rather sadly admiring her charcoal drawings which decorate the walls. One figure has a grin. She smudges out the grin and adds a 'sad' mouth. She turns to Ruth.

Bronia   What you doing with our sheets, Ru?
Ruth   I want to make a cover for the gap in the wall. Edek will bring us better sheets anyway, and we've got to stop the draught somehow.   *(To herself)*   Trouble is I haven't got a needle. I suppose I'll have to make one from a splinter.

(Bronia is balancing a stick of charred wood on her fingers. Finally she drops it. She drags her feet over to where Ruth is sitting and drapes her arms around Ruth's neck from behind.)

Bronia   How long have we been living in this cellar, Ruth?
Ruth   Don't know, love — but look, at least we're safe here. The Nazis haven't got time to come searching across this side of the city for three lost kids.

(Pause. Bronia moves away and sits on a box opposite Ruth. She bites her fingernails.)

Ruth   *(A little sharp)*   Don't do that, Bron!

(Bronia starts to cry.)

Ruth   *(Exasperated)*   Oh, Bronia, pull yourself together: I only *spoke* to you.

Bronia   Please, Ruth, I don't know what to *do*. I'm fed up with this place. I don't like the rats. I want Mummy and Daddy to come back!

Ruth   *(Crosses to her)*   I'm sorry. I know it's not much fun for you. It's no joke for me either. Edek will be back soon. He's gone to the Polish Council to try to find out about Mum.   *(She looks round rather hopelessly)*   Why don't you do some more drawing?

Bronia   *(Desperately)*   There's no more wall left, Ru!

(Ruth sees this is true. She is moved by a surge of compassion for her little sister. She hugs Bronia and swings her on to a box. She sits down next to her, confidentially.)

Ruth   I know what we'll do! We'll do what we always did. Starting tomorrow you are going to *school*!

Bronia   *(Amazed)*   Where, Ruth?

Ruth   Here, in this very room. We'll have our own school. Your friends from the street can come. I'm old enough to be your teacher. It'll do you all good. They can bomb every building in Warsaw, but it won't stop children learning how to add up and take away. And if there are no reading books . . . well, we'll have to *tell* each other stories!

(She begins to be carried away by her own ideas, pacing up and down the cellar. Bronia just sits and stares, wide-eyed.)

Ruth   We'll have lessons in the morning only. Plenty of time for play in the afternoon. We'll start with a Bible story — I shall have to remember carefully. Then arithmetic or writing. Then a break. We can do games and PE on the open site when there's not a raid —

(Edek enters. She stops abruptly. There is a silence.)

Edek   *(Forced cheerfulness)*   I got some bread at the convent.   *(Silence)*   And I fixed up a job at the soup-kitchen. One of the boys was run in for theft . . .   *(He breaks off)*

Ruth   Edek!

(He can hide it no longer. He sits looking at audience. Ruth and Bronia move to him.)

Edek   They said Mum was taken to Germany to work on the land. But they can't say where.

(Blackout 5 seconds.)

SCENE 2

Joseph   *(Narrator)*   In the summer they left the city for the woods. Life was healthier there. They lived under an oak tree. When it rained, they got wet. When the sun shone it browned their limbs.

      Because of the kindness of the peasants, food was more plentiful. It was forbidden to store food or to sell to anyone but the Nazis, but they gave the children whatever they could spare.

      They hid it too, in cellars, in haystacks, in holes in the ground. With the help of the older children they smuggled it to the towns and sold it on the black market. Edek was a good smuggler. Ruth and Bronia were well fed, for he was well paid.

    *(**Improvisation**   Edek barters with Peasant over barrow-load of filled logs which he is to take to the Peasant's accomplice in the market; ends with Edek forcing price up.)*

Peasant   OK. OK. You're good. It's dangerous. Two rye loaves, apples and butter. Under the cattle trough in the top field tomorrow. Leave the cart in the first barn.

(They shake hands on it. Exit Peasant. Edek pushes away barrow, stops and turns to audience.)

Edek   At school they taught me how to
        Play the game
        Follow the rules
        'Honest' was my middle name

        But now I know the two-faced world
        More than I did before
        Some rules are only for the rich
        And others for the poor

        To those who have, to them
        Shall all the more be given
        God bless the helpless
        Their reward's in heaven!

        Don't tell me that I'm cheating now
        I know the score:
        Trust yourself, trust no-one else:
        Their game is war.

(Edek pushes the barrow round in a circle. As he returns he meets a crowd — the market. Two German Soldiers enter. Edek, whistling, almost runs into them.)

Soldier 1   'Ello what 'ave we 'ere then?
Soldier 2   Goin' somewhere, young man?
Soldier 1   Anythin' to declare?
Soldier 2   Anythin' we ought to know about?
Soldier 1   Got a pretty sister at 'ome?
Soldier 2   Get on wiv me mate, would she?
Soldier 1   What's on yer wagon, mate?

Soldier 2   Logs in summer?
Soldier 1   Suspicious!
Soldier 2   Most suspicious!
Soldier 1   'Ave a look shall we?
Soldier 2   Wouldn't be tryin' t' pull a fast one, eh?
Soldier 1   Stop us seein' the wood for the trees?

(Soldiers begin to examine the logs. Edek is off, like a rabbit. He dodges among the crowd who obstruct the Soldiers. He makes his escape up some steps. The Soldiers stop at the bottom.)

Soldier 1   'E's got away!
Soldier 2   Yeah — I know 'im, 'e's slippery as an eel. But I got 'im marked down — we'll get 'im next time.

(They disappear into shadow.)

SCENE 3

Cellar interior: Ruth is standing before the 'class' of ragged school children.

Ruth   So although the king knew he had been tricked, he had to go through with it. He called for Daniel and sent him into the den. And he rolled a huge stone over the entrance of the den and sealed it himself. Then he went back to his palace, but he couldn't sleep, thinking about Daniel, wondering if the lions would devour him. Well, when morning came, he rushed out and rolled back the stone and there stood Daniel, all in one piece, with the lions dozing quietly around him. And Daniel said: 'O King live forever, my God has sent an angel who shut the lions' mouths and they have not hurt me.'

(She stops, sighs, satisfied.)

Eva   *(After a pause)*   Please, Ruth — Miss — are you going to tell us what the story means?

(Others murmur 'Yes — you always tell us . . . ' etc.)

Ruth   Why don't you tell me, Eva? Your meaning is as good as anyone else's.

(Eva looks down at her feet.)

Ruth   *(Smiles)*   Don't worry, Eva.   *(Pause)*   Well, sometimes I think of it as the story of our own troubles. The lions are: cold and hunger and hardship. But if only we are patient and trustful like Daniel, we will be delivered from them . . .   *(She falters)*   Sometimes though I see the lions scowling and snarling. . . .   *(Snapping out of it)*   No! never mind that. We've been in this damp cellar too long this morning. Out you go everybody: into the sun!

*(***Improvisation***   The children play 'Air-raid alert'. Ruth remains in cellar. While attention is focused on game Jan drags himself close to edge of stage and collapses unseen.)*

Bronia   *(Runs towards Jan, sees him, stops, approaches him cautiously. After a pause)*   Ruth, Ruth, there's a boy lying down outside and he won't get up.
Ruth   Tickle his ribs!
Bronia   I don't think he can get up.
Ruth   Who is it?
Bronia   It's not one of the class. I've never seen him before.

(Ruth goes to investigate.)

Ruth   *(To the children who have gathered round)*   Does anyone know who he is?   *(They shake their heads.)*
Ruth   He looks ill and starved. Yankel, will you help me lift him down to the cellar? And, Eva, please find something for him to drink, some milk if you can get it.

(They move him to centre stage. Jan calls for his pet 'Where's Jimpy?' One of the children fetches a crate with the cockerel from Jan's point of entrance. Jan calls the name again.)

Ruth   That's a fine name, what's yours?

(Eva returns with cup.)

Ruth   All right you others, I think this young man needs a rest. Off you go and play again.   *(They do so reluctantly.)*
(To Jan)   Look, Eva's brought some milk for you. Sit up and drink it. You'll feel better in a minute.

(Jan sits up and drinks. Bronia comes back, whispers to Ruth.)

Bronia   *(To others)*   He still won't tell us his name!
Kate   *(Brings Jan's box)*   I found this in the street where he was lying. I think it must be his.
Bronia   *(Snatching box)*   It's heavy and it rattles. He must be rich! Ruth, may we undo the string?
Ruth   *(With authority)*   Give the box to him. Nobody shall touch it without asking him.

(Jan takes the box and smiles. The children clamour to find out what's inside.)

Jan   *(Holding the box out of reach)*   No-one sees into my treasure box. But since you gave it back to me I'll tell you my name. It's Jan.
Ruth   *(Holds out her hand)*   I'm Ruth, this is my sister Bronia. These children are from the street. They go to our school.   *(Jan looks puzzled)*   We live here in the cellar. There used to be three of us, but my brother Edek went out smuggling one day and never came back.

(She looks across to where Edek appears momentarily and is arrested by the two Soldiers who have been waiting in the shadows. They search him and discover food being smuggled inside his coat.)

Ruth   Perhaps you will help us find him again. Perhaps now you have come we shall be lucky.

(Lights to half on stage. Spot upon Joseph, narrator.)

Joseph   For some days Jan was too ill to leave. What he needed was rest, warmth and good solid food. Ruth was a good nurse. The children left him alone, but they scrounged for him what they could for food. By the time Jan was better he didn't want to go.
    Edek had gone; Jan had arrived. The Germans went; the Russians arrived. Several streets away there appeared a brand new hut — a Russian control post . . .

Questions

1　Why does Ruth think the children are safe from the Nazis?

2　Why does Bronia begin to cry?

3　What, according to Edek, has happened to his mother?

4　Where did the children live when they left the city?

5　How were the children able to get food?

6　'Wouldn't be trying' t' pull a fast one, eh?' What do the German soldiers suspect Edek of doing?

7　What does Edek do when the German soldiers begin to examine the logs?

8　In what condition is Jan found?.

9　What does Ruth do to help Jan get well?

10　Why does Jan decide to tell the children his name?

11　Which character did you like most from these scenes? Why?

12　What kind of scenery would you need if you were putting on this play for a public performance?

AROUND THE WORLD

7

NOVELS

Undersea Adventure

Erika has a series of unusual experiences while she is swimming below the surface of the sea surrounding her island home of Rongo.

Like a small fish I flitted through that monstrous foliage, for no leaves on earth are longer than kelp leaves. Where the sunlight filtered, they showed cloudy yellow and brown. Nature had arranged that gas-filled bulges in their structure held them upright in the water so they could get light and oxygen near the surface. Because of this, so did the forest's inhabitants — sponges, squids, lobsters, sea snails and little fish that lived like birds in the boughs.

I floated dreamily, watching a shadow rising from the blue depths, a dark blur. The shark came straight up, almost under my feet, and the disturbance of its arrival tossed me into the kelp. I have to tell this fast, because it must have happened all in the space of a breath, the one I had in my lungs. But it is true that time stretches. Hours and days passed, and left me with a lifetime memory. I hung amongst the leaves hearing my heart lurch back and forth, afraid the shark would hear it too. But it quietly floated there, the faintest curl of its tail flukes keeping it steady. Perhaps it scented me. It was as big and round as a large barrel, and four times longer than I. It was built of gristle and black leather. Its eye was circular darkness surrounded by china white. A fish scuttled by, and lazily the shark took it, the entire jaw coming forward smoothly, out beyond the lips. Like a machine, a machine with an appetite.

I was a nothing, a titbit, sifted down from the sea's surface, hiding with burning lungs amongst the shifting kelp. My only thought was that if I breathed out, the creature would see the bubbles and charge into the kelp after me. But was it a thought? Rather knowledge, handed down from hundreds of generations of sea-people. If I had any choice, it was between drowning where I clung, or shooting up to the surface and being eaten on the way. No, I did no thinking. My whole body and mind were one enormous yell: 'Help me, I'm going to die.'

The pain in my chest was too great to bear. Red lightning shot across my eyeballs; everything seemed red; I knew some part inside me must burst. Then the sea erupted. Something hurtled past me like a black rocket, tearing the waters apart, jerking the kelp from the seafloor, hurling me away into furious cascades, waterspouts, exploding light, roaring air — air that rushed into my body and out again with a whoop. There I lay, limp amongst the limp kelp, muscles wrenched, half-dead, but half-alive also, and not knowing how or why.

Feebly I thought that the shark had indeed attacked me and somehow I had survived. I tried to swim, to flee, but my arms were lead. All I could do was drag myself over a huge hollow stem and collapse in a trance of shock and fatigue.

While I lay there, I heard a whale blow, whahhhhhhhh! A shower of fine warm mist descended on me. Laboriously turning my head, I saw the whale nearby, half submerged. I saw the blowhole, a huge black leather dimple, trembling as she breathed; her eye, tucked above the long sweep of her upper jaw; her warty brow; the waves slapping over her peaked spine and dorsal fin as if she were a half-tide rock. That whale was keeping an eye on me.

I knew the shark had fled. The whale had heard my mind shrieking for help and had come to my aid. She was the Aunt — I recognised her by a barnacle as big as a dinner plate on her upper lip. It must have been painful. Weakly I thought: 'Stig will get that off for you.'

She moved nearer. Perhaps she was curious about the little creature, so ill-shaped, so unskilled in the sea. Beneath me I saw the long winglike flipper, the scalloped edge, the white dents of old wounds and barnacle sores. Shakily I reached out to touch it, and it was warm like a paw, or my own hand. Tears rushed out of my eyes.

I can't describe what love rushed out of me with those tears. I wanted everything that was good for that old whale — a long life, wide wanderings in sweet seas, no wicked ship sneaking up on her to send an exploding harpoon into her guts to blow heart and lungs to pulp.

'I wish I could make it different for you, for all the whales!' I thought, and the answer came in the dolphins' word, in Dockie's — shah, shah, be at peace, little child.

I thought then of the infant whale she must have recently seen born, floating belly up, its mother going around it in mournful circles. Somehow I was not surprised to know it had been born dead.

Shock is very strange. In a kind of way a shocked person is asleep, for when I awakened — if awaken I did — the whale was gone, and I was surrounded and supported by dolphins. She must have called them in from the ocean, knowing that she could not take me into the shallow water where I would be safe. They passed me from one to the other, whistling shrilly; sometimes I lay across a back, other times I held to a warm strong tail. At one moment, I know, I rode my friend Emere, for Sif later told me that is what they saw when she and Henry, having heard the furious commotion of the whale's attack on the shark, rowed around the point of the bay.

'The sea was boiling with dolphins,' Sif said. 'I've never seen so many in one place. They pushed you up into the shallows with their snouts. I thought one or two of them might well have stranded. But the queerest thing of all was that there was a whale out in the deep water, lying still as a reef, as if she were watching. Then up came her tail and she dived.'

As Henry and Sif ran the dinghy up the sand, and jumped to help me, the dolphins fled to deep water and stood on their tails in the way they have, creaking anxiously. I tottered to my feet like a rickety cat and fell into Henry's arms. It was the safest, most comforting place I had been for years.

from *My Sister Sif* by Ruth Park

Reading for Meaning

1 What is Erika doing at the beginning of her story?

2 What was the first indication Erika had of the shark's presence?

3 How do you know the shark arrived very quickly?

4 What did the shark do once it had appeared?

5 How big was the shark?

6 Why did Erika believe that the shark was 'a machine with an appetite'?

7 Why do you think Erika's lungs were burning?

8 Why didn't Erika breathe out?

9 What choices did Erika appear to have?

10 'Red lightning shot across my eyeballs; everything seemed red . . .' What do you think was causing this?

11 'I tried to swim, to flee . . .' Why couldn't Erika escape?

12 'A shower of fine warm mist descended on me.' What caused this?

13 What did the whale's flipper feel like?

14 What kind of life did Erika want the whale to have?

15 Why, according to Erika, had the dolphins arrived?

16 What is the meaning of 'the sea was boiling with dolphins'?

17 How did the dolphins bring Erika to safety?

18 What did the dolphins do when Henry and Sif came to help Erika?

The Polar Bear

Alone in the Canadian Arctic, Matthew and his Eskimo friend, Kayak, narrowly escape a deadly confrontation with a huge polar bear.

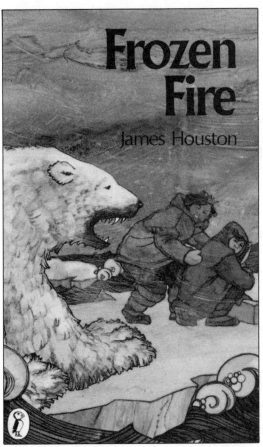

'Come and help me,' Matthew called to Kayak.

'Don't move,' answered Kayak in a whisper. There was terror in his voice.

Cautiously Matthew turned and saw the white head and black beady eyes as it moved snakelike through the icy water. When it reached the small ice pan on which they stood, the huge polar bear heaved its bulk out of the water and shook itself like an immense dog. It looked yellow against the stark white snow.

Matthew saw the great bear swing its head back and forth, sniffing the air suspiciously. Its huge blue-black mouth hung open showing its terrible teeth. With a rumbling growl,

the giant bear lowered its head and came shambling towards them.

Matthew and Kayak lay like dead men on the ice, both their heads turned so that they could watch the bear. Matthew clutched the snow knife like a dagger and trembled inside, as he felt the wet salt water seep up from the snow and soak his clothing.

The bear did not even pause to look at them, as it stalked past. They saw it crouch down flat against the snow.

Cautiously Matthew looked ahead and saw a seal's dark head poised alert and motionless in the water. The bear was watching it intently.

Seeing nothing move to frighten it, the seal

relaxed and let its back float to the surface as it drew a large breath of air into its lungs and dove beneath the ice in search of food.

The bear snaked forward cautiously until it reached the very edge of the ice where it had seen the seal. It reached out its paw and scratched against the ice.

The seal must have heard the sound beneath the water and, being curious, it once more raised its head above the surface. Seeing nothing but a yellowish heap of snow, it swam cautiously along the edge of the ice.

Suddenly, with lightning swiftness, the bear's right paw shot out and struck the seal's head a killing blow. The left paw lunged forward and hooked the seal inward with its great curved claws. Using its teeth, the bear easily hauled the hundred-pound seal up onto the ice pan.

Matthew watched it sniff the dead seal all over, then roll it on its back and, holding it steady, tear its throat open with its powerful jaws. It started to devour its prey.

'Stay still,' Kayak hissed through his teeth, now chattering from cold and fear.

At last Matthew saw that the big bear was finished eating. They watched it as it licked its lips and, like a huge cat, carefully wiped the seal fat from its mouth. It turned and shambled towards them, paused and sniffed the air. With its belly rumbling, it padded once more to the edge of the ice and slipped silently into the freezing water. Kayak sat up carefully as the bear swam south. They saw it climb up on another pan and amble off, disappearing into the whirling snow.

Kayak rolled stiffly onto his hands and knees, then crouched like an animal, still watching the place where they had last seen the bear.

from *Frozen Fire* by James Houston

Reading for Meaning

1 Why was there terror in Kayak's voice when he whispered 'Don't move.'?

2 What did the bear do immediately after it had heaved itself out of the water?

3 What was terrifying about the bear's appearance?

4 What did Matthew and Kayak do when the bear came towards them?

5 'They saw it crouch down flat against the snow.' Why did the bear 'crouch down flat'?

6 Why was the seal relaxed?

7 What was the seal doing?

8 How did the bear cause the seal to come to the surface again?

9 Why didn't the seal notice the bear?

10 How did the bear kill the seal?

11 How did the bear get the seal out of the water?

12 What did the bear do after it had sniffed the dead seal all over?

13 Why were Kayak's teeth chattering?

14 Where did the bear go after it had slipped into the water again?

15 Did you find this an exciting story? Why or why not?

The Hurricane

Here is a graphic description of the assault of a hurricane on an isolated Pacific village. The 'bures' mentioned in the passage are the traditional thatched cottages of the region.

On the morning of the thirty-fifth day of drought, the sun rose red over a great bank of black cloud, and a wind blew in from the sea, smelling of rain. People staggered half-asleep from their bures and stood facing the wind, laughing like small children. Such clouds they'd never seen before. They were higher than mountains and as wide as the island, dark as the depths of night. At last the sun was returning all the water it had stolen.

But as they watched, the wind grew stronger. Within minutes the sea was swept into white-peaked waves that burst into foam on the beach. Palms creaked, groaned, and bent their leaves. The village was shrouded in dust and flying leaves.

The people hurried back to their bures. The wind had whipped the smiles from their faces, and their voices were shrill with alarm. This was the beginning of a hurricane.

Even as they tried to close the thatched shutters, the wind hit with full force and tore the fastenings from their hands. The air screamed into their bures as though it were full of attacking demons, which choked and blinded them with dust.

Families crouched in fear and held on to

one another, heads bowed, while walls bent toward them and the thatch of roofs peeled away. Outside they could hear the death sounds of trees, shrieks of splintered wood, then thumps, as the green giants of their village were ripped from the ground.

The rain came with the same murderous fury, not rain at all but a torrent of dark water, which burst against the village like a tidal wave, soaking the bures in seconds and pouring down the inside walls. It climbed cold around the ankles of terrified men and women who tried to hold their children beyond its reach. They screamed and prayed but couldn't hear the sounds of their own voices. Their ears were full of the noise of wind and water and terrible thunder. White fire lit the fear on their faces, flash after flash of lightning. The forked tongue of the Snake God Degei brought punishment to his people. His voice called for their destruction.

In the darkness of Luisa's bure, three people huddled against the strongest wall, waiting for death. Samu was as speechless as Jonasi, and Luisa by now was so frightened she could neither cry nor pray. The black water rose around their legs and was flowing so fast that the bure would have been swept away had it not been built against a strong tree, which in turn was protected by other trees.

It was not the wind and rain that Luisa dreaded, but the water they stood in. It was salt. That could mean only one thing: the sea was rising to cover the land.

Because of the turtle. She was sure of it now. Everything because of that turtle.

But the sea rose no higher than their ankles. As time passed, so did the hurricane. Late in the afternoon the wind lessened and gradually died until the rain fell straight to earth. The sea retreated.

It was nearly over.

Tired, silent people waded through the water that flowed across their village and looked at the desolation. Everywhere there was wreckage. The torrent had swept banks of debris against uprooted trees, forming dams, and against one of these was the body of a pig. The other pigs, still tethered by their legs, were also dead. The goats and hens had disappeared.

It would be a long time before they would have more copra. Those palms that hadn't

fallen were stripped of nuts and most of their leaves. One canoe lay on its side in the middle of the village where the cooking fire had been; the others had been swept away.

Everything was choked with thick yellow mud.

The people had been delivered from one fear to another. Now they had water, plenty of water, but hunger was much closer than it had been the day before.

They splashed around their bures trying to rescue their few possessions, sleeping mats, a little food, a wooden bowl here, a cooking pot there — doing what they could to repair damage before nightfall. Some of the bures were still intact, some required more work than could be done in a day. But only one had been completely destroyed.

The home of Bulai had been swept away.

Bulai and his wife were safe. At the height of the storm the wind had lifted their roof, first a corner, then the whole thing. Bulai had dragged his wife out into the screaming darkness to the next bure, and only just in time. Another great gust and the walls twisted and collapsed. When the hurricane died, there wasn't a trace of the house they'd lived in. It had all been swept out to sea.

from *The Silent One* by Joy Cowley

Reading for Meaning

1 What indication did the people have that the rain was coming?

2 What was unusual about the clouds?

3 What is the meaning of: 'At last the sun was returning all the water it had stolen'?

4 What effect did the wind have on the sea?

5 What happened as the islanders tried to close the thatched shutters?

6 What were the families doing inside their bures?

7 'Outside they could hear the death sounds of trees.' What was happening to the trees?

8 Why couldn't the villagers hear the sounds of their own voices?

9 'White fire lit the fear on their faces, flash after flash of lightning.' Explain what is happening.

10 What saved Luisa's bure from destruction?

11 Why did Luisa dread the water she was standing in?

12 What happened late in the afternoon?

13 'Everywhere there was wreckage.' What wreckage did people find?

14 Why would it be a long time before the villagers would have more copra?

15 In what way were the people 'delivered from one fear to another'?

16 What did the people do after the storm?

17 How had Bulai saved his own and his wife's life?

POETRY

PEOPLE AND PLACES

from Everest Climbed

Their steps were weary, keen was the wind,
Fast vanishing their oxygen fuel,
And the summit ridge was fanged and cruel —
Fanged and cruel, bitter and bare.
And now with a sickening shock
They saw before them a towering wall
Of smooth and holdless rock.
O ghastly fear — with the goal so near
To find the way was blocked!
On one side darkly the mountain dropped,
On the other two plunging miles of peak
Shot from the dizzy skyline down
In a silver streak.

'No hope of turning the bluff to the west,'
Said Hillary. 'What's that I see to the east?
A worm-wide crack between cornice and rock —
Will it hold? I can try it at least.'
He called to Tenzing, 'Draw in the slack!'
Then levered himself right into the crack
And, kicking his spikes in the frozen crust,
Wriggled up with his back.
With arms and feet and shoulders he fought,
Inch by sweating inch, then caught
At the crest and grabbed for the light of day.
There was a time, as he struggled for breath, to pray
For all the might that a man could wish —
Then he heaved at the rope till over the lip
Brave Tenzing, hauled from the deep, fell flop
Like a monstrous gaping fish.

Was the summit theirs? — they puffed and panted —
No, for the ridge still upward pointed.
On they plodded, Martian-weird
With pouting mask and icicle beard
That crackled and tinkled, broke and rattled,
As on with pounding hearts they battled,
On to the summit —
Till at last the ridge began to drop.

Two swings, two whacks of Hillary's axe,
And they stood on top.

Ian Serraillier

Questions

1 What words at the beginning of the poem show the tiredness of Hillary and Tenzing?

2 What was the summit ridge like?

3 How did Hillary and Tenzing feel when they saw the 'towering wall'?

4 What is the meaning of 'holdless rock'?

5 What was the 'goal' of Hillary and Tenzing?

6 What hope was there for Hillary 'to the east'?

7 'Like a monstrous gaping fish'. Why does the poet compare Tenzing to a fish?

8 Why do Hillary and Tenzing appear 'Martian-weird'?

9 What sounds did their beards make?

10 What were some of the difficulties that Hillary and Tenzing had to overcome while climbing Mount Everest?

11 What does this poem reveal about the characters of Hillary and Tenzing?

12 What other title could you give this poem?

Cockpit in the Clouds

Two thousand feet beneath our wheels
The city sprawls across the land
Like heaps of children's blocks outflung,
In tantrums, by a giant hand.
To east a silver spire soars
And seeks to pierce our lower wing.
Above its grasp we drift along,
A tiny, droning, shiny thing.

The noon crowds pack the narrow streets.
The el trains move so slow, so slow.
Amidst their traffic, chaos, life,
The city's busy millions go.
Up here, aloof, we watch them crawl.
In crystal air we seem to poise
Behind our motor's throaty roar —
Down there, we're just another noise.

Dick Dorrance

Space Pilot

The land sinks back
The rockets shoot their bolt,
Earth's pull weakens and dies.
I breach space and become a celestial body,
Moving with planets and suns
Through darkness, silence and cold,
But having no place in this void
My weight lost, my breath in an envelope
My eyes replaced by intricate instruments.
There is no place for the heart.
Here, needing the light and the seasons.
But the soul perhaps?
Released from all that I could not carry with me
I shall stare unhindered into the face of God.

John Blackie

Releasing a Migrant 'Yen' (Wild Goose)

At Nine Rivers, in the tenth year, in winter, — heavy snow;
The river-water covered with ice and the forests broken with their load.
The birds of the air, hungry and cold, went flying east and west;
And with them flew a migrant 'yen', loudly clamouring for food.
Among the snow it pecked for grass; and rested on the surface of the ice;
It tried with its wings to scale the sky, but its tired flight was slow.
The boys of the river spread a net and caught the bird as it flew;
They took it in their hands to the city-market and sold it there alive.
I that was once a man of the North am now an exile here:
Bird and man, in their different kind, are each strangers in the south.
And because the sight of an exiled bird wounded an exile's heart,
I paid your ransom and set you free, and you flew away to the clouds.

Chinese poem, translated by *Arthur Waley*

Questions

1 What effect has winter had on the land?

2 Why did the birds of the air go 'flying east and west'?

3 Why did the 'yen' land on the ice?

4 How was the bird captured?

5 What did the boys do with the bird?

6 Why were the bird and man 'strangers in the south'?

7 What did the man do with the bird after he bought it?

8 What did the bird do when it was set free?

9 Why do you think the man set the bird free?

10 What did you learn about the character of the poet from your reading of this poem?

Friendly Fauna

Welcome to Australia!
You must come and meet
our cuddly native animals,
timorous and sweet.
This vast and wondrous country,
where creatures rare abound —
Oops! Did it bite you,
that black snake on the ground?
I really should have warned you
to take care how you tread,
for twined around your other foot
I see a copperhead.
What pretty coloured berries!
Ah, Nature! Great Provider!
Sorry, my mistake —
do not eat that red-back spider!
Yes, of course you may paddle
you may certainly go in,
but I wouldn't get too pally
with that sinister black fin!
You've changed your mind?
You'd rather have a safe and gentle stroll
among these sparkling rock pools —
get your hand out of that hole!
Phew! A blue-ringed octopus
was lurking by that rock!
And, by the way, a funnel web
is crawling up your sock.
What? You want to leave already,
when there's bushland still to see,
with charming little animals,
as shy as they can be.
There's one now — but watch it!
Oh dear, I should have said:
Tassie devils can turn nasty
if you pat them on the head.
It's a shame you've lost your fingers.
Yes, I guess you do feel weak.
But I still haven't shown you
the bunyip in the creek!

Robin Klein

Questions

1 What kind of native animals does the poet want the visitor to Australia to 'come and meet'?

2 Why does the poet say 'I really should have warned you/to take care how you tread'?

3 What is hidden in the 'pretty coloured berries'?

4 What danger is there in the sparkling rock pools?

5 'It's a shame you've lost your fingers'. Why has this happened?

6 What has the poet revealed about Australia in this poem?

7 Do you think the poet exaggerates in her poem? Why?

8 What have you learned about the poet's personality from your reading of this poem?

9 Why do you think the poet has called her poem 'Friendly Fauna'?

10 Did you think this poem was humorous or serious? Explain your viewpoint.

The Miner

There are countless tons of rock above his head,
And gases wait in secret corners for a spark;
And his lamp shows dimly in the dust.
His leather belt is warm and moist with sweat,
And he crouches against the hanging coal,
And the pick swings to and fro,
And many beads of salty sweat play about his lips
And trickle down the blackened skin
To the hairy tangle on the chest.
The rats squeak and scamper among the unused props,
And the fungus waxes strong

Idris Davies

WRITING

WRITING AN ESSAY

When you come to write an essay, it is important that you organise your thoughts and ideas so that your essay has a structure. A simple structure that will work for most pieces of writing consists of:

An **introduction**, made up of a sentence or a short paragraph in which you bring to the attention of your reader the topic or subject you are going to write about.

The **main part** or **body** of your piece of writing — two or more paragraphs in length.

The **conclusion**. This is a paragraph or sentence that sums up or completes your piece of writing.

INTRODUCTION

↓

MAIN PART
or
BODY

↓

CONCLUSION

Now look at how Colin Thiele, a famous Australian writer, has set out his description of the death of the magpie, Mate, in his novel *Magpie Island*. In the first paragraph he describes the setting and the characters. In the next two paragraphs he develops the action of the story, and in the last paragraph he describes the tragic death of Mate.

THE DEATH OF MATE

Introduction
Bert Whiting, from Port Lincoln, was flying his spotter plane on a big sweep west towards the Bight to see if he could pick up an early sign of tuna. But how was Mate

to know that? It was a lovely morning, the sea a pattern of twinkles and herringbone, and the sky as blue and delicate as the shell of a starling's egg. Bert felt happy. He swung his plane about in the empty air, pretending to dive-bomb his shadow. He felt like a wartime flying ace. He saw the island up ahead and decided to strafe all the hidden gunners in the caves on the cliffs.

Body

He opened the throttle until the engine roared, and dived down steeply towards the shore. The wind whistled past the wings. Just as it seemed that he was going to crash straight into the black rocks he levelled out to shoot fast and low over the lip of the island. Too late, he saw the colony of terns. They rose up in a screaming cloud right in front of him, thousands of them, like white confetti thrown upwards. In a second or two he would be plunging into the middle of them, blinded, windshield smashed, plane out of control. So at the last instant he banked hard to starboard, pulling grimly, desperately. The engine shrieked. The plane, missing the outriders of the terns by fractions, levelled over the island, its wings hissing so low that the grass streamed and flattened in its wake.

Mate heard it coming. If only she had stayed where she was, crouched low and safe while it rushed overhead!

Conclusion

But the monster was too terrifying and her fear was too great. She could feel it upon her. The air was shuddering and shattering, the ground trembling, the grass tearing in tumult. She couldn't stand it any longer. She had to escape, to fly, to fly. She leapt from the tussock where she crouched, and flapped frantically upwards. The wings and fuselage of the plane missed her as she rose, but the tail-plane struck her with all its fury. There was a puff of feathers, and then Mate's body was hurled back by the slip-stream, tumbling over and over as it fell, until it was carried past the edge of the cliffs' into the swirling water below. There it lay for a second like a bundle of old rags and then sank from sight for ever. Mate was dead.

From *Magpie Island* by Colin Thiele

Your Turn to Write

Now, using the simple structure you have been given, write an essay on one of the following topics.

- The phone call I should never have answered
- The day I was involved in a road accident
- An embarrassing happening
- Never again!
- How I feel when I'm sick
- It was the best day of my life
- A terrifying experience
- Memories

LANGUAGE

ADJECTIVES

Adjectives describe people or things. An adjective adds colour, shape, size, strength, feeling or some other quality to a noun. Good writers use adjectives to make their writing come alive. Look at these examples from *Frozen Fire*. The adjectives are in heavy type.

- It looked **yellow** against the **stark, white** snow.
- With a **rumbling** growl, the **giant** bear lowered its head.
- Suddenly, with **lightning** swiftness, the bear's right paw shot out.

Adjectives are found everywhere. Look at the 'Hagar' cartoon and see how many adjectives you can find in the riddle.

Adjectives in Action

Charles Dickens, a famous nineteenth-century English writer, used adjectives to great effect in his novels. Write down his description of a convict from *Great Expectations* and underline the adjectives.

THE CONVICT

This man . . . had a great iron on his leg, and was lame, and hoarse, and cold, and was everything that the other man was; except that he had not the same face, and had a flat, broad-brimmed, low-crowned felt hat on.

Now read through the poem 'Girls' by John Cunliffe. It is a poem full of adjectives describing girls at school. Write down the poem and underline at least ten of the adjectives.

Girls

We've all sorts of girls in our school:
Bony,
Podgy,
Giggly,
Dodgy,
Sickly smiley,
Shampooed and shiny,
Smelly wellies,
Big and busty,
Dirty dusty;
All sorts . . .
Some pretty ones, too . . .
One or two really nice ones . . .
Well . . . one, just one . . . really special one.
BUT
the one I really hate,
Is Miss Whisper-behind-her-hand.
She gives me a smooth look,
Snooty;
Then she whispers to her Special Friend,
And I know it's something nasty,
. . . about me.

John Cunliffe

Essential Adjectives

Here are some important adjectives that are constantly used in everyday life. Add the missing letters and give the meaning of each adjective.

1 perman _ nt
2 conceit _ d
3 cowardl _
4 diffic _ lt
5 viol _ nt
6 delic _ _ us
7 irr _ table
8 comf _ rtable
9 danger _ _ s
10 exc _ ll _ nt

11 fasc _ n _ ting
12 essent _ al
13 victor _ _ us
14 pleas _ nt
15 terrif _ _ d
16 sympath _ t _ c
17 innoc _ nt
18 remark _ ble
19 caref _ l
20 horr _ ble

21 energ _ t _ c
22 slipp _ ry
23 fierc _
24 corr _ ct
25 neglig _ nt
26 cauti _ _ s
27 beaut _ f _ l
28 destr _ ct _ ve
29 disguis _ d
30 fer _ cious

Identifying Adjectives

Similes use adjectives to create comparisons. Write down each of these animal and bird similes and underline the adjectives. The first one has been done to help you.

Animal Similes
1 as slow as a tortoise
2 as hungry as a wolf
3 as gentle as a lamb
4 as cunning as a fox
5 as fat as a pig
6 as strong as an ox
7 as slippery as an eel
8 as obstinate as a mule
9 as poor as a church mouse
10 as sick as a dog

Bird Similes
1 as wise as an owl
2 as swift as a hawk
3 as graceful as a swan
4 as proud as a peacock
5 as gentle as a dove
6 as plump as a partridge
7 as happy as a lark
8 as tender as a chicken
9 as talkative as a magpie
10 as black as a raven

Adjectives Similar in Meaning

Replace the adjectives in italic type with adjectives from the box that are similar in meaning.

fierce	feeble	brave	short
accurate	quick	gigantic	sufficient
courteous	empty	invincible	shining
industrious	rich	annoyed	invaluable

1 *priceless* diamond

2 *ferocious* dog

3 *precise* answer

4 *angry* teacher

5 *busy* worker

6 *unbeatable* army

7 *valiant* soldier

8 *enough* food

9 *weak* attempt

10 *brief* visit

11 *vacant* house

12 *wealthy* developer

13 *prompt* reply

14 *huge* wave

15 *gleaming* light

16 *polite* child

Adjectives and Their Opposites

Match up the adjectives in the left-hand column with their opposites in the right-hand column.

private	innocent
false	happy
fresh	wise
noisy	expensive
foolish	true
rough	stale
guilty	senior
cheap	selfish
junior	public
humble	quiet
miserable	proud
generous	smooth

PUNCTUATION

APOSTROPHES — TO CONTRACT WORDS

In speaking and in writing we often contract or shorten two words and use them as one word. One use of the apostrophe is to indicate where letters have been left out.

For example:

- **He's** left   (He has left)
- She **wouldn't** come   (She would not come)

Using Apostrophes

Use an apostrophe to write the contracted form of each of the following.

1 We are not afraid.

2 I am ready.

3 You are next.

4 We will not go.

5 It is his fault.

6 He must not fail.

7 She is clever.

8 I did not see you.

9 They were not there.

10 He could not win.

11 They had finished.

12 She would not participate.

Using the Complete Form

Write down the full form of each of the following.

1 We'll be coming.

2 I've finished.

3 He couldn't hear.

4 Here's my number.

5 I don't know.

6 They won't be going.

7 They'd already left.

8 Who's ready?

9 We're present.

10 Didn't you hear the bell?

11 You'd have laughed.

12 What's the time?

DRAMA

GROUP ACT-OUTS

Form groups and act out these situations. It's a good idea to spend a lesson or more discussing and practising what you are going to say and do. You may even like to prepare a script.

HIJACKED

Everything is quiet aboard the Boeing 747 as the passengers of Flight 2000 from London to Rome are settling in their seats for a comfortable journey. Suddenly the anguished voice of the pilot, Captain Stewart, is heard over the intercom. 'This is your captain speaking. This aircraft has been hijacked. Do not move from your seats. Do as you are told. The hijackers are armed with submachine guns and grenades. They are at this moment entering the passenger area of the plane. They will soon give you your orders. Please listen carefully. Your safety depends on this. Over and out.'

CHARACTERS

Captain Stewart	Hijacker 1 (Leader)	Passenger 1
Co-pilot	Hijacker 2	Passenger 2
Flight Attendant 1	Hijacker 3	Passenger 3
Flight Attendant 2	Hijacker 4	Passenger 4
Flight Attendant 3	Hijacker 5	Passenger 5

AFTER THE NUCLEAR WAR

There has been a nuclear holocaust. All the major cities around the world have been destroyed. Twelve people are fighting for their survival in a nuclear fallout shelter on the outskirts of a major city. The tension in the shelter is great as the survivors have to endure the problems of food rationing and living together in a confined space for a period of six weeks. When they decide to emerge from the shelter, they are appalled by the sights that confront them. The world as they have known it has been destroyed. Yet, despite the desolation that surrounds them, they are determined to establish a new life.

CHARACTERS

Jenny Wang, aged 28, computer expert
Andrew Hudson, aged 49, doctor
Ben Harper, aged 34, soldier
Laura Wetherall, aged 53, teacher
John Rogers, aged 40, builder
Sally Rogers, aged 36, housewife
Julie Rogers, aged 14, student
Ben Rogers, aged 10, student
Peter Riemer, aged 32, minister
Christine Howarth, aged 22, sports professional
Alex Sanderson, aged 68, pensioner
Georgina Swartz, aged 56, secretary

ON THE LEDGE

A crowd is gathered beneath an office block in New York where Robert Andrews is threatening to jump from a ledge on the tenth floor. Sam Stuart, a police officer, notices the man on the ledge and alerts the police department and the fire brigade. The police arrive and take over the tenth floor. A number of people — Robert's wife, his father, his mother, a psychiatrist, a police sergeant and a priest — try to persuade Robert not to jump. What happens?

CHARACTERS

Robert Andrews
Sam Stuart
Robert's wife

Robert's father
Robert's mother
a psychiatrist

a police sergeant
a priest
police officers

IN TROUBLE WITH THE PRINCIPAL

Four pupils are waiting outside the principal's office to be punished for offences they have committed. Each pupil, in turn, tells the others why he or she is in trouble. They are then called in by the principal. Act out the scenes that occur outside and inside the principal's office.

CHARACTERS

Timothy   Sue
Debbie   the principal
Andrew

THAT'S
INCREDIBLE

8

NOVELS

Annabel's Amazing Story

Annabel Andrews is the name of the teenager telling this story.

You are not going to believe me, nobody in their right minds could *possibly* believe me, but it's true, really it is!

When I woke up this morning, I found I'd turned into my mother. There I was, in my mother's bed, with my feet reaching all the way to the bottom, and my father sleeping in the other bed. I had on my mother's night-gown, and a ring on my left hand, I mean her left hand, and lumps and pins all over my head.

'I think that must be the rollers,' I said to myself, 'and if I have my mother's hair, I probably have her face, too.'

I decided to take a look at myself in the bathroom mirror. After all, you don't turn

into your mother every day of the week; maybe I was imagining it — or dreaming.

Well, I wasn't. What I saw in that mirror was absolutely my mother from top to toe, complete with no braces on the teeth. Now ordinarily, I don't bother to brush too often — it's a big nuisance with all those wires — but my mother's teeth looked like a fun job, and besides, if she was willing to do a terrific thing like turning her body over to me like that, the least I could do was take care of her teeth for *her*. Right? Right.

You see, I had reason to believe that she was responsible for this whole happening. Because last night, we had a sort of argument about something and I told her one or two things that had been on my mind lately.

As a matter of fact, if it's OK with you, I think I'd better start back a little farther with some family history, or you won't know what I'm talking about or who (whom?).

My name is Annabel Andrews. (No middle name, I don't even have a nickname. I've been trying to get them to call me Bubbles at school, but it doesn't seem to catch on.) I'm thirteen; I have brown hair, brown eyes, and brown fingernails. (That's a joke — actually, I take a lot of baths.) I'm five feet; I don't remember what I weigh but I'm watching it, although my mother says it's ridiculous, and I'm not *completely* mature in my figure yet. Maybe by the summer though.

My father is William Waring Andrews; he's called Bill; he's thirty-eight; he has brown hair which is a little too short, but I've seen worse, and blue eyes; he's six feet (well, five eleven and a half); and he's a fantasti-

cally cool person. He's an account executive at Joffert and Jennings, and last year his main account was Fosphree. If you're into the environment thing at all, you know what that is: no phosphates, low sudsing action, and, according to my mother, grey laundry. We had boxes of the stuff all over the kitchen. You couldn't *give* it away. This year, he has New Improved Fosphree (That's what they think!), plus something called Francie's Fortified Fish Fingers. *Barf* time! If there's anything more disgusting than fortified fish, I don't know what.

Oh yes, I do, I just thought of what's worse. My brother. He is I cannot begin to tell you how disgusting. It may not be a nice thing to say but, just between you and me, I *loathe* him. I'm not even going to bother to describe him — it's a waste of time. He looks like your average six-year-old with a few teeth out, except that, as my grandmother keeps saying, 'Wouldn't you know it'd be the boy who gets the long eyelashes and the curly locks? It just doesn't seem fair.' No, it certainly doesn't, but then what's fair? These days, not much. Which is exactly what I was trying to tell my mother last night when we had the fight. I'll get to that in a minute, but first a few facts about Ma.

Her name is Ellen Jean Benjamin Andrews, she's thirty-five — which makes her one of the youngest mothers in my class — she has brown hair and *brown* eyes. (We're studying Mendel. I must be a hybrid brown. With one blue- and one brown-eyed parent you're supposed to get two brown-eyed kids and two blue-eyed kids. So far there are only two kids in our family, but look who's already got stuck with the brown eyes. Me. The sister of the only blue-eyed ape in captivity. That's what I call him. The blue-eyed ape. Ape Face for short. His real name is Ben.) Anyway, back to my mother. Brown hair, brown eyes, and, as I've already mentioned, nice straight teeth which I did *not* inherit, good figure, clothes a little on the square side; all in all, though, she's prettier than most mothers. But *stricter*.

That's the thing. I can't stand how strict she is. Take food, for instance. Do you know what she makes me eat for breakfast? Cereal, orange juice, toast, an egg, milk, and two Vitamin C's. She's going to turn me into a blimp. Then for lunch at school, you have one of two choices. You can bring your own bag lunch, with a jelly sandwich or a TV dinner (They're quite good cold.) and a Coke, or if you're me, you have to eat the hot meal the school gives you, which is not hot and I wouldn't give it to a dog. Alpo is better. I know because our dog eats Alpo and I tried some once.

She's also very fussy about the way I keep my room. Her idea of neat isn't the same as mine, and besides, it's my room and I don't see why I can't keep it any way I want. She says it's so messy *nobody* can clean in there,

but if that's true, how come it looks all right when I come home from school? When I asked her that last night, she just sighed.

A few other things we fight about are my hair — she wants me to have it trimmed but I'm not falling for that again (The last time it was 'trimmed' they hacked six inches off it!) — and my nails which I bite.

But the biggest thing we fight about is freedom, because I'm old enough to be given more than I'm getting. I'm not allowed to walk home through the park even with a friend, because 'New York is a very dangerous place and especially the park.' Everybody else's mother lets them, 'but I'm not everybody else's mother.' You're telling me!

Tomorrow one of my best friends in school who lives in the Village is having a boy-girl party and she won't let me go because last time that friend had a party they played kissing games. I told her the mother was there the whole time, staying out of the way in the bedroom, of course, and she said, 'That's exactly what I mean.'

What kind of an answer is that? I don't get it. I don't get any of it. All I know is I can't eat what I want, wear what I want, keep my hair and my nails the way I want, keep my room the way I want or go where I want. So last night we really had it out.

'Listen!' I screamed at her. 'You are not letting me have any fun and I'm sick of it. You are always pushing me around and telling me what to do. How come nobody ever gets to tell *you* what to do, huh? Tell me that!'

She said, 'Annabel, when you're grown-up, people don't tell you what to do; you have to tell yourself, which is sometimes much more difficult.'

'Sounds like a picnic to me,' I said bitterly. 'You can tell yourself to go out to lunch with your friends, and watch television all day long, and eat marshmallows for breakfast and go to the movies at night . . .'

'And do the laundry and the shopping, and cook the food, and make things nice for Daddy and be responsible for Ben and you . . .'

'Why don't you just let me be responsible for myself?' I asked.

'You will be, soon enough,' she said.

'Not soon enough to suit me,' I snapped.

'Is that so!' she said. 'Well, we'll just see about that!' and she marched out of the room. All of which should explain why I wasn't as surprised as most people would be if they woke up in their mother's body.

from *Freaky Friday* by Mary Rodgers

Reading for Meaning

1 How does Annabel seize your interest at the beginning of her story?

2 What evidence did Annabel have for believing she had turned into her mother?

3 Why doesn't Annabel brush her teeth very often?

4 Why does Annabel think her mother is responsible for the change?

5 What is Annabel's attitude to her father?

6 Why are there boxes of Fosphree all over the Andrews' kitchen?

7 What are Annabel's feelings towards her brother?

8 What complaint does Annabel's mother make about Annabel's room?

9 Why doesn't Annabel want her hair trimmed?

10 What is the biggest thing Annabel and her mother fight about?

11 Why isn't Annabel allowed to walk home through the park?

12 Why won't Annabel's mother let her go to the 'boy-girl' party?

13 According to Annabel, what are the advantages of being a grown-up?

14 According to Annabel's mother, what are some of the disadvantages she has as a parent?

15 Do you think Annabel's mother is being too strict with Annabel? Gives reasons for your viewpoint.

16 What comments would you make about Annabel's character?

The Defeat of the Tripod

This story takes place a hundred years from now in a land ruled by the dreaded Tripods, sixty-foot-high moving machines.

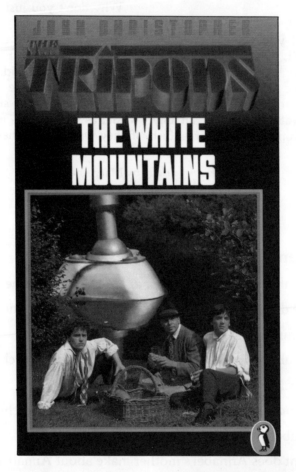

I felt the ground shiver under me, and again and again with still greater force. Then one of the Tripod's legs plunged across the blue, and I saw the hemisphere, black against the arc of sky, and tried to dig myself down into the earth. At that moment the howling stopped. In the silence I heard a different, whistling sound of something whipping terribly fast through the air and, glancing fearfully, saw two or three bushes uprooted and tossed away.

Beside me, Beanpole said: 'It has us. It knows we are here. It can pull the bushes out till we are plainly seen.'

'Or kill us, pulling them out,' Henry said. 'If that thing hit you . . .'

I said: 'If I showed myself . . .'

'No use. It knows there are three.'

'We could run different ways,' Henry said. 'One of us might get away.'

I saw more bushes sail through the air, like confetti. You do not get used to fear, I thought; it grips you as firmly every time. Beanpole said:

'We can fight it.'

He said it with a lunatic calm, which made me want to groan. Henry said:

'What with? Our fists?'

'The metal eggs.' He had his pack open already, and was rummaging in it. The Tripod's tentacle whistled down again. It was ripping the bushes up systematically. A few more passes — half a dozen at most — would bring it to us. 'Perhaps these were what our ancestors used, to fight the Tripods. Perhaps that is why they were in the underground Shmand-Fair — they went out from there to fight them.'

I said: 'And they lost! How do you think . . .?'

He had got the eggs out. He said: 'What else is there?'

Henry said: 'I threw mine away. They were too much trouble to carry.'

The tentacle sliced into the bushes, and this time we were scattered with earth as it pulled them up. Beanpole said:

'There are four.' He handed one each to Henry and me. 'I will take the others. If we pull out the rings, count three, then stand up and throw. At the leg that is nearest. The hemisphere is too high.'

This time I saw the tentacle *through* the bushes as it scooped up more. Beanpole said: 'Now!'

He pulled the rings from his eggs, and Henry did the same. I had taken mine in my left hand, and I needed to transfer it to the right. As I did so, pain ripped my arm-pit again, and I dropped it. I was fumbling on the ground to pick it up when Beanpole said 'Now!' again. They scrambled to their feet, and I grabbed the last egg, ignoring the pain of the movement, and got up with them. I ripped out the ring just as they threw.

The nearest foot of the Tripod was planted on the slope, thirty yards or so above us. Beanpole's first throw was wild — he did not get within ten yards of his target. But his second throw, and Henry's, were close to the mark. One of them hit metal, with a clang that we could hear. Almost at once they exploded. There were three nearly simultaneous bangs, and fountains of earth and dust sprouted into the air.

But they did not obscure one plain fact: the eggs had done no damage to the Tripod. It

stood as firmly as before, and the tentacle was swishing down, this time directly towards us. We started to run, or rather, in my case, prepared to. Because before I could move, it had me round the waist.

I plucked at it with my left hand, but it was like trying to bend a rock. It held me with amazing precision, tight but not crushing, and lifted me as I might lift a mouse. Except that a mouse could bite, and I could do nothing against the hard gleaming surface that held me. I was lifted up, up. The ground shrank below me, and with it the figures of Beanpole and Henry. I saw them darting away like ants. I was steeple-high, higher. I looked up, and saw the hole in the side of the hemisphere. And remembered the iron egg still clutched in my right hand.

How long was it since I had pulled the ring out? I had forgotten to count in my fear and confusion. Several seconds — it could not be long before it exploded. The tentacle was swinging me inwards now. The hole was forty feet away, thirty-five, thirty. I braced myself back, straining against the encircling band. Pain leapt in my arm again, but I ignored it. I hurled the egg with all my strength, and what accuracy I could muster. I thought at first that I had missed, but the egg hit the edge of the opening and ricocheted inside. The tentacle continued to carry me forwards. Twenty feet, fifteen, ten . . .

Although I was nearer, the explosion was not as loud as the others had been, probably because it happened inside the hemisphere. There was just a dull, rather hollow bang. Despair came back: that was my last chance gone. But at that instant I felt the metal holding me relax and fall away.

I was three times the height of a tall pine; my bones would smash against the ground when I landed. I clutched desperately at the thing against which, a few seconds earlier, I had been struggling. My hands gripped the metal, but I was falling, falling. I looked at the ground, and closed my eyes as it rushed up to meet me. And then there was a jerk which almost tore me from my hold, and the falling stopped. My feet shivered, a few inches from the surface. All I had to do was let go, and step down.

The others came to me. We stared up, in awe, at the Tripod. It stood there, seemingly unharmed. But we knew it was finished, destroyed, lifeless.

from *The White Mountains* by John Christopher

Reading for Meaning

1 What was the first indication the storyteller had of the Tripod's presence?

2 What did the storyteller do when he saw the Tripod?

3 Why was the Tripod removing the bushes?

4 What was Henry's plan?

5 How did Beanpole think they could fight the Tripod?

6 Why had Henry thrown his eggs away?

7 What do you think the metal eggs might be?

8 How do you know that the storyteller had been hurt previously?

9 How successful was Beanpole's first throw?

10 How do you know the first three eggs had done no damage to the Tripod?

11 Why wasn't the storyteller able to run away with Beanpole and Henry?

12 What evidence can you find to show that the storyteller was lifted very high into the air?

13 Why didn't the storyteller know how long it was since he had pulled the ring out?

14 '. . . I felt the metal holding me relax and fall away.' Why did this happen?

15 Why did the storyteller think his bones would smash against the ground when he landed?

16 What comments would you make about the characters of Beanpole, Henry and the storyteller?

In the Land of the Little People

When Gulliver's ship is wrecked in a storm, he is washed up on a strange beach. He finds himself in the land of Lilliput.

It was morning when I woke and tried to get up. But something strange had happened while I was asleep. I could not move an inch. My arms and legs were now tied down to the ground and even my hair, which was long and thick, had been tied down with string so that I could not move my head to see what had happened to me. All around me was the hum of little voices — but I could see nothing except the empty sky. I knew there were people around me, but as far as my eyes could reach there was no one to see.

As I lay there, frightened and puzzled, there was a movement on my left leg. Something alive was moving up my body towards my chin. It felt like a large insect and I looked anxiously down to see what was coming. It came into sight and there I could see a tiny man, less than six inches high, marching up my chest with a bow and arrow in his hand. I could hardly believe my eyes. But after him came forty more little men who marched up my body as though it was a battlefield.

In my fright at seeing these astonishing people I cried out so loudly that all the little men ran away. Many of them were hurt jumping from my side down to the ground but soon the others came back and climbed over me again. One of the bravest came far enough to see my face and called out to his friends with admiration. I could not understand his language, however, and my fright increased. Struggling hard, I was able to free my left arm and to loosen my hair a little so that I could turn my head. Before I could seize them, all the little people ran away and a hundred arrows hit my hand like needles. Others fell on my face so that I cried out with pain and fought to get free. More arrows came, however, and at last I decided it was safer to lie still.

As soon as I was quiet the soldiers stopped shooting arrows at me, but more and more little people were joining the crowd around me. Now that I could move my head a little I could see hundreds of workmen building a stage about eighteen inches high, near my right ear. I watched them working and was amazed by their skill and speed. Though they were no bigger than my thumb these people seemed able to do everything that men of our own size can do.

When the stage was finished a well-dressed man, who seemed to be an important officer, climbed to the top with three servants. From there he was able to speak directly into my ear and leaning towards me he made a long speech. I could not understand one word, of course, but from the repetition of the name 'Lilliput' I guessed that this must be the name of the country to which I had come. Later I learned that this was correct.

The officer's manner seemed friendly and when he had finished I felt less frightened. I was very hungry, however, and I put my finger in my mouth to show that I needed food. At once the officer understood me and shouted orders to his men. Soon ladders were placed at my side and a hundred little men climbed up to my mouth with baskets of food. The meat and the vegetables looked much like our own food, but everything was very small. I took two or three baskets at a mouthful and then ate some loaves of bread which were smaller than marbles. They brought me barrels of water which were no larger than nuts and the little people were so amazed at the number of barrels that I drank that they danced on my chest with excitement.

It would have been easy now to seize forty or fifty men and throw them to the ground, but as I had tasted their food and drink I felt I was now their guest. More and more I admired their bravery in coming so close to me. Now another official came up my chest and showed me a piece of paper smaller than my thumbnail. It seemed to be important, but I did not understand then that it was an order from the King of Lilliput that I should be taken to his capital city, which was called Mildendo. As I did not know of this plan I did not worry about it. Instead I began to feel very sleepy because the little people had put in my water a medicine to make me sleep. Now they loosened a little the ropes that tied me and they put more medicine on the places where their poisoned arrows had hurt me. I felt more comfortable when this had been done and soon I fell asleep again.

from *Gulliver's Travels* by Jonathan Swift

Reading for Meaning

1 Why couldn't Gulliver (the storyteller) move an inch?

2 How did Gulliver know that there were people around him?

3 What did the little man moving up Gulliver's body feel like?

4 What did the little men do when Gulliver cried out loudly?

5 What did one of the bravest men do?

6 Why did Gulliver cry out with pain?

7 When did the soldiers stop shooting arrows at Gulliver?

8 Why was Gulliver amazed by the workmen building the stage?

9 Why was the well-dressed man able to speak directly into Gulliver's ear?

10 Why did Gulliver think 'Lilliput' was the name of the country?

11 How did Gulliver indicate that he was hungry?

12 Why did the little people dance on Gulliver's chest with excitement?

13 Why did Gulliver decide not to seize forty or fifty of the little people and throw them to the ground?

14 What order did the King of Lilliput give concerning Gulliver?

15 Why did Gulliver begin to feel sleepy?

16 How did the author, Jonathan Swift, create the impression in this passage that Gulliver was a giant compared to the people of Lilliput?

POETRY

Wanted — A Witch's Cat

Wanted — a witch's cat.
Must have vigour and spite,
Be expert at hissing,
And good in a fight,
And have balance and poise
On a broomstick at night.

Wanted — a witch's cat.
Must have hypnotic eyes
To tantalize victims
and mesmerize spies,
And be an adept
At scanning the skies.

Wanted — a witch's cat,
With a sly, cunning smile,
A knowledge of spells
And a good deal of guile,
With a fairly hot temper
And plenty of bile.

Wanted — a witch's cat,
Who's not afraid to fly,
For a cat with strong nerves
The salary's high
Wanted — a witch's cat;
Only the best need apply.

Shelagh McGee

The Haunting of Wicked McNaught

There's a terrible tale that's told
Of a castle in the Glen
Haunted by McNaught of Naughton
The wickedest of men.
He died whilst fighting twenty soldiers
Single handed twelve he slew
Until a razor-edged Claymore
Cut his strong right leg in two
Now from the crypt and full red-bearded
Every night at the stroke of ten
He hops out looking for his lost leg
That's said to roam the glen.

Passing travellers swear they've seen it
Hopping round the castle grounds
With McNaught close behind it
As it jumps in leaps and bounds
He tries with might and main to catch it
But it stays one jump ahead
And screaming like a man demented
He beats his big fists on his head
And cries, 'I curse the curse I'm cursed with
How can I do evil work
When the tartan sock I'm chasing's
Where I keep my little dirk?'

Along the battlements, down stairwells
Through the big hall, servants' quarters
Then the chase across the drawbridge
Mirrored in the moat's dark waters
To that battleground so fatal
To the spot where he was slain
There he grabs it by the ankle,
And sticks it on again
Then with an evil roar of triumph
He cries, 'My missing leg I've found'
And then a voice calls out from Heaven,
It's on the wrong way round.

Jeremy Lloyd

Kenneth

who was too fond of bubble-gum and met an untimely end.

The chief defect of Kenneth Plumb
Was chewing too much bubble-gum.
He chewed away with all his might,
Morning, evening, noon and night,
Even (oh, it makes you weep)
Blowing bubbles in his sleep.
He simply couldn't get enough!
His face was covered with the stuff.
As for his teeth — oh, what a sight!
It was a wonder he could bite.
His loving mother and his dad
Both remonstrated with the lad.
Ken repaid them for their trouble
By blowing yet another bubble.

'Twas no joke. It isn't funny
Spending all your pocket money
On the day's supply of gum —
Sometimes Kenny felt quite glum.
As he grew, so did his need —
There seemed no limit to his greed:
At ten he often put away
Ninety-seven packs a day.

Then at last he went too far —
Sitting in his father's car,
Stuffing gum without a pause,
Found that he had jammed his jaws.
He nudged his dad and pointed to
The mouthful that he couldn't chew.
'Well, spit it out if you can't chew it!'
Ken shook his head. He couldn't do it.
Before long he began to groan —
The gum was solid as a stone.
Dad took him to a builder's yard;
They couldn't help. It was too hard.
They called a doctor and he said,
'This silly boy will soon be dead.
His mouth's so full of bubble-gum
No nourishment can reach his tum.'

Remember Ken and please do not
Go buying too much you-know-what.

Wendy Cope

Questions

1 What was Kenneth's chief defect?

2 What did Kenneth do in his sleep?

3 'Sometimes Kenneth felt quite glum'. Why was this so?

4 How much bubble-gum did Kenneth 'put away' at ten?

5 What happened to Kenneth while he was sitting in his father's car?

6 What was his father's advice to Kenneth?

7 Why couldn't the people in the builder's yard help Kenneth?

8 Why did the doctor think that Kenneth would soon be dead?

9 What examples of exaggeration can you find in the poem?

10 Do you think this poem is funny or serious? Explain your opinion.

The Late Express

There's a train that runs through Hawthorn
3 a.m. or thereabout.
You can hear it hooting sadly,
but no passengers get out.

'That's much too early for a train,'
the station-master said,
'but it's driven by Will Watson
and Willie Watson's dead.'

Poor Willie was a driver
whose record was just fine,
excepting that poor Willie
never learnt to tell the time.

Fathers came home late for dinner,
schoolboys late for their exams,
millionaires had missed on millions,
people changing to the trams.

Oh such fussing and complaining,
even Railways have their pride —
so they sacked poor Willie Watson
and he pined away and died.

Now his ghost reports for duty,
and unrepentant of his crime,
drives a ghost train through here nightly
and it runs to Willie's time.

Barbara Giles

Questions

1 What is unusual about the 3 a.m. train through Hawthorn?

2 What was wrong with Willie's record as a driver?

3 What problem did Willie cause fathers?

4 What problem did Willie cause schoolboys?

5 Why do you think there was 'fussing and complaining'?

6 What did the Railways do about Willie?

7 What then happened to Willie?

8 What is the meaning of 'unrepentant of his crime'?

9 What is the meaning of 'it runs to Willie's time'?

10 Why is the poem called 'The Late Express'?

The Old Wife and the Ghost

There was an old wife and she lived all alone
    In a cottage not far from Hitchin:
And one bright night, by the full moon light,
    Comes a ghost right into her kitchen.

About that kitchen neat and clean
    The ghost goes pottering round.
But the poor old wife is deaf as a boot
    And so never hears a sound.

The ghost blows up the kitchen fire,
    As bold as bold can be;
He helps himself from the larder shelf,
    But never a sound hears she.

He blows on his hands to make them warm,
    And whistles aloud 'Whee-hee!'
But still as a sack the old soul lies
    And never a sound hears she.

From corner to corner he runs about,
    And into the cupboard he peeps;
He rattles the door and bumps on the floor,
    But still the old wife sleeps.

Jangles and bang go the pots and the pans,
    As he throws them all around;
And the plates and the mugs and dishes and jugs,
    He flings them all to the ground.

Madly the ghost tears up and down
    And screams like a storm at sea;
And at last the old wife stirs in her bed —
    And it's 'Drat those mice,' says she.

Then the first cock crows and morning shows
    And the troublesome ghost's away.
But oh! what a puckle the old wife sees
    When she gets up next day.

'Them's tidy big mice,' the old wife thinks,
    And off she goes to Hitchin,
And a tidy big cat she fetches back
    To keep the mice from her kitchen.

James Reeves

Questions

1 When did the ghost come into the old wife's kitchen?

2 Why doesn't the old wife hear a sound?

3 What does the ghost do to show he is 'As bold as bold can be'?

4 What noise does the ghost himself make?

5 What noises do the pots and pans make?

6 What does the ghost do with the plates and mugs?

7 When does the old wife finally stir?

8 What did the old wife think was making the noises?

9 When does the ghost go away?

10 What does the old wife fetch back from Hitchin?

WRITING

EMOTIONS

Each day we experience all kinds of feelings or emotions. Surprise, joy, jealousy, sadness, fear, loneliness and excitement are just a few of them. Betsy Byars is expert in describing situations involving human emotions. In the first passage, from her novel *The Eighteenth Emergency*, notice how she describes the scene involving Benji's fear of Marv Hammerman and Tony Lionni. In the second passage, from her novel *The Pinballs*, Betsy Byars' character, Carlie, feels that all the world is against her. She in turn is antagonistic towards all those she comes into contact with.

Fear

The pigeons flew out of the alley in one long swoop and settled on the awning of the grocery store. A dog ran out of the alley with a torn Cracker Jack box in his mouth. Then came the boy.

The boy was running hard and fast. He stopped at the sidewalk, looked both ways, saw that the street was deserted and kept going. The dog caught the boy's fear, and he started running with him.

The two of them ran together for a block. The dog's legs were so short he appeared to be on wheels. His Cracker Jack box was hitting the sidewalk. He kept glancing at the boy because he didn't know why they were running. The boy knew. He did not even notice the dog beside him or the trail of spilled Cracker Jacks behind.

Suddenly the boy slowed down, went up some steps and entered an apartment building. The dog stopped. He sensed that the danger had passed, but he stood for a moment at the bottom of the steps. Then he went back to eat the Cracker Jacks scattered on the sidewalk and to snarl at the pigeons who had flown down to get some.

Inside the building the boy was still running. He went up the stairs three at a time, stumbled, pulled himself up by the banister and kept going until he was safely inside his own apartment. Then he sagged against the door.

His mother was sitting on the sofa, going over some papers. The boy waited for her to look up and ask him what had happened. He thought she should be able to hear something was wrong just from the terrible way he was breathing. 'Mom,' he said.

'Just a minute. I've got to get these orders straight.' When she went over her cosmetic orders she had a dedicated, scientific look. He waited until she came to the end of the sheet.

'Mom.' Without looking up, she turned to the next page. He said again, '*Mom.*'

'I'm almost through. There's a mistake some —'

He said, 'Never mind.' He walked heavily

through the living-room and into the hall. He threw himself down on the day bed.

His mother said, 'I'm almost through with this, Benjie.'

'I said, "Never mind".' He looked up at the ceiling. In a blur he saw a long cobweb hanging by the light fixture. A month ago he had climbed on a chair, written UNSAFE FOR PUBLIC SWINGING and drawn an arrow to the cobweb. It was still there.

He closed his eyes. He was breathing so hard his throat hurt.

'Benjie, come back,' his mother called. 'I'm through.'

'Never *mind*.'

'Come on, Benjie, I want to talk to you.'

He got up slowly and walked into the living-room.

She had put her order books on the coffee table. 'Sit down. Tell me what's wrong.' He hesitated and then sat beside her on the sofa.

She waited and then said again, 'What's wrong?'

He did not answer for a moment. He looked out of the window, and he could see the apartment across the street. A yellow cat was sitting in the window watching the pigeons. He said in a low voice, 'Some boys are going to kill me.'

'Not *kill* you, Benjie,' she said. 'No one is —'

He glanced quickly at her. 'Well, how do I know what they're going to do?' he said, suddenly angry. 'They're chasing me, that's all I know. When you see somebody chasing you, and when it's Marv Hammerman and Tony Lionni and a boy in a black sweat shirt you don't stop and say, "Now, what *exactly* are you guys planning to do — kill me or just break a few arms and legs"?'

'What did you do to these boys?'

from *The Eighteenth Emergency* by Betsy Byars

Resentment

Carlie had been suspicious of people since the day she was born. She swore she could remember being dropped on the floor by the doctor who delivered her.

'You weren't dropped,' her mother had told her.

'All right then, why is my face so flat? Was I *ironed*?'

Carlie also claimed that when she was two months old a baby-sitter had stolen a golden cross from round her neck.

'No baby-sitter stole a gold cross from you,' her mother had told her.

'All right then, where is it?'

Carlie believed everyone was out to do her in, and she had disliked Mrs Mason, the foster mother, as soon as she had seen her standing in the doorway.

'I knew she'd have on an apron,' Carlie said to the social worker. 'She's trying to take off Mrs Walton — unsuccessfully, I might add.'

'Maybe she has on the apron because she was cooking, Carlie.'

'*I* should be the social worker. I'm not fooled by things like aprons.'

She also didn't like the Masons' living-room. 'This is right out of "Leave It to Beaver",' she said. She especially distrusted the row of photographs over the fireplace. Seventeen pictures of — Carlie guessed — seventeen foster children.

'Well, my picture's not going up there,' she grumbled to herself. 'And nobody had better snap me when I'm not looking either.' She sat.

Mrs Mason waited until 'Young and Restless' was over and then she said, 'Carlie?'

'I'm still here.'

'Well, come on and have some lunch. Then afterwards you can help me get the boys' room ready.'

Carlie turned. She looked interested for the first time. 'The boys?' she asked. 'There're going to be some boys here?'

'Yes, two boys are coming this afternoon — Thomas J. and Harvey.'

'How old?'

'Eight and thirteen.'

'Oh, boo, too young.' Carlie got up from the footstool. 'What's wrong with them?'

'Wrong with them?'

'Yeah, why do they have to be here? I'm here because I got a bum stepfather. What's their trouble?'

'Well, I guess they'll have to tell you that.'

Carlie lifted her hair up off her neck. 'How about the thirteen-year-old?' she said. 'What's he like. Big for his age, I hope.'

'He has two broken legs. That's about all I can tell you.'

'Well,' Carlie said, 'that lets out dancing.'

from *The Pinballs* by Betsy Byars

YOUR TURN TO WRITE

Select one of the following topics and describe a situation involving your feelings.

- sadness
- holidays
- spiders
- winning a lottery
- lost
- being angry
- sunrise
- sunset
- fishing
- sharks
- winning
- losing
- food

- romance
- having fun
- loneliness
- exams
- movies
- love
- friendship
- hate
- winter
- summer
- spring
- Christmas
- last lesson Friday

- fear
- at the dentist
- in hospital
- money
- a happy birthday
- surprise
- snakes
- sight-seeing
- picnics
- going for a walk
- excursions
- music
- sunbathing

LANGUAGE

ADVERBS

As their name suggests, adverbs add to the meaning of verbs. Usually you can identify a word as an adverb by testing to see whether it answers the questions *how?*, *when?* or *where?* asked about a verb. Adverbs often end in 'ly'.

Adverbs That Tell How

Example: I clutched **desperately** at the Tripod.

The adverb 'desperately' tells us *how* the storyteller clutched at the Tripod.
  Other examples are: happily, fast, angrily, rapidly, smoothly.

Adverbs That Tell When

Example: A few seconds **earlier**, I had been struggling against it.

The adverb 'earlier' tells us *when* the storyteller had been struggling against the Tripod.
  Other examples are: previously, soon, often, then, again.

Adverbs That Tell Where

Example: The Tripod's tentacle whistled **down**.

The adverb 'down' tells us *where* the Tripod's tentacle whistled.
  Other examples are: here, there, everywhere, locally, nearby.

Writers use adverbs to heighten the interest level of their writing. For example:

- **Suddenly** I felt weak. *(The Midnight Fox)*
- **Cautiously** Matthew turned and saw the white head and black beady eyes. *(Frozen Fire)*
- It stood there **seemingly** unharmed. *(The White Mountains)*
- **Slowly** I turned on to my hands and knees. *(Dragon in the Garden)*

Forming Adverbs of Your Own

Most adverbs are formed by adding 'ly' to an adjective. Complete these sentences by changing the word in the brackets to an adverb ending in 'ly'. Note that sometimes you will need to add or change other letters as well.

1 They were behaving .... (strange)

2 He reached for the knife .... (frantic)

3 We fought .... (brave)

4 He followed .... (faithful)

5 You conducted your business .... (successful)

6 The clouds disappeared .... (sudden)

7 She was .... ill. (extreme)

8 We left .... (immediate)

9 You swam .... (slow)

10 He was .... in trouble. (constant)

11 I wrote .... (careful)

12 They won .... (easy)

13 The letter arrived .... (unexpected)

14 She .... climbed the ladder. (cautious)

15 They attended the meetings .... (frequent)

Adverbs and Their Meanings

Write down the following sentences, replacing the phrases in italics with adverbs from the box

1 I will meet you *at this place*.
2 We will have to leave *in a short time*.
3 He came to the hospital *every day*.
4 They walked *at a rapid pace*.
5 He failed the test *over and over again*.
6 The florist arranged the flowers *with care*.
7 We must leave *at once*.
8 They awaited the results *with patience*.
9 He searched *every possible place*.
10 The swimmer completed the race *with ease*.

easily
repeatedly
carefully
everywhere
here
patiently
immediately
daily
soon
briskly

Appropriate Adverbs

Choose the most suitable adverbs from the boxes and insert them in the sentences. Each adverb may only be used once.

yesterday	tomorrow	nearby	very	fast

1 The car was travelling extremely ....
2 They are leaving for home ....
3 He lives ....
4 .... we went to the cinema.
5 The traveller was .... tired.

courageously	tightly	rapidly	restlessly	hoarsely

1 The fire was beginning to spread ....
2 He tossed .... in his sleep.
3 The carpenter screwed the two pieces of wood together ....
4 The crowd was shouting .... during the last few minutes of the game.
5 The young soldier fought .... against the enemy.

Adverbs and Their Opposites

Match up the adverbs on the left with their opposites on the right.

falsely   sadly
externally   calmly
carefully   seldom
late   internally
heavily   wearily
angrily   truly
often   accidentally
happily   carelessly
energetically   early
deliberately   lightly

Adverb Stories

Here are two stories for you to complete using adverbs of your own.

The Robbery
The thief broke the window ....
He entered the room ....
.... the burglar alarm went off.
The thief picked up his tools ....
He raced .... to escape through the window.
He jumped .... into the garden below.
.... he was captured by the police.

Danger in the Surf
The swimmer called .... for help.
Hearing the cry, the lifesaver scanned the sea ....
He .... saw the frantic swimmer.
Diving into the waves, he swam .... out to the swimmer.
The swimmer .... allowed himself to be rescued and taken to the beach.

Now write your own adverb story for other members of the class to complete.

PUNCTUATION

THE APOSTROPHE — TO SHOW POSSESSION

The apostrophe is used to show possession (or ownership) in the following ways:

- If the noun that possesses is *singular*, add an apostrophe then an 's'.
  Example: The girl's blouse. (The blouse of the girl)

● If the noun that possesses is *plural* and already ends with 's', add an apostrophe.

Example: The girls' blouses. (The blouses of the girls)

● If the noun that possesses is *plural* but does not end with 's', add an apostrophe then an 's'.

Example: The women's dresses. (The dresses of the women)

Using the Apostrophe to Show Ownership

Use the apostrophe to show ownership in each of the following.

Example: the horns of the cow = the cow's horns

1 the homework of the student

2 the wings of the birds

3 the tusks of the elephant

4 the cars of the teachers

5 the food of the baby

6 the crown of the prince

7 the home of the woman

8 the wall of the church

9 the signal of the motorist

10 the noise of the children

11 the dresses of the ladies

12 the roofs of the houses

13 the teeth of the crocodile

14 the yelping of the dogs

15 the coats of the men

16 the speed of the horses

DRAMA

The Fantastic Failures

by Robert Hood

CHARACTERS

Dragular   a vampire
Harriet   a head-hunter
Crossbones   a skeleton
Eh?   a genie
Zee-Zee   a zombie
Aloysius   an alien
Wendy   a werewolf
Professor Mandrake   headmaster of Horror Hall Preparatory
   School For Terribly Nasty Monsters
Raven Maniac   a mad killer
Donald Horror-Gruesome-Sicko Pus-Monster the Third

The auditorium of Horror Hall Preparatory School For Terribly Nasty Monsters. There are seats around the wall and a big banner saying 'Welcome, Monster Class of 1980'. There is also a table with drinks etc.

Dragular, Crossbones, Harriet and Eh? are sitting apart from each other, looking nervous.

Dragular   *(To Harriet)*   Hello . . . um, I mean, guten tag!
Harriet   Hi!
Dragular   You do not look like a monster! You vere in ze class of 1980, ja? Vot did *you* graduate as?
Harriet   A head-hunter. My name's Harriet. What about you?
Dragular   Eine vampire, of course. Call me Dragular. But tell me vot you do. You decapitate person's heads, ja?
Harriet   Well, sort of . . . yeah, that's what I do. I'm . . . um, really nothing special.
Dragular   Tell me, ist zere lots of blood ven you do zat?
Harriet   Of course. Lots.
Dragular   *(Looking sick)*   Oh, dear.

Harriet   But you don't want to hear about me.

Crossbones   Sufferin' catfish! Stop being so coy! Just tell us about yaself. That's what we're 'ere for, ain't it?

Harriet   I beg your pardon?

Crossbones   We're 'ere to tell each other how flamin' successful we are, ain't we?

Harriet   *(Aside)*   I hope not.   *(To Crossbones)*   I know you! You're Crossbones Jones! You were always skinny . . . but you've really become anorexic, haven't you!

Crossbones   A pirate skeleton, that's me. Cursed to forever guard gold doubloons . . . that sort of thing!

Dragular   Vot do you do?

Crossbones   Mostly I hang around sunken ships and strangle anyone who comes along lookin' for treasure.

Harriet   Have you strangled anyone recently?

Crossbones   Well . . . of course. I mean, what do ya think I am? A deviant or something?

Harriet   Sorry.

Crossbones   Well, are ya gonna tell us about yaself?

Harriet   I told you, I'm a head-hunter. You know, savage, inhuman rituals . . . voodoo curses . . . slicing the heads off innocent victims and . . . um, piling them up to form a temple to the evil demon . . . what's-'is-name?

Crossbones   I don't know.

Harriet   I always forget it.   *(She changes the subject, turning to Dragular)*   Tell us what it's like being a vampire. All that blood, and midnight tombs, and biting people in the neck?

Dragular   Vell, you know, is really exciting.

Harriet   Yes?

Dragular   Vell, you've zeen ze mooffies, nein? I in graveyards lurk . . . unt . . . um, vell, vait for ein victim . . . zomevun nice unt juicy . . . unt bite zem in ze neck.

Crossbones   S'pose ya turn into bats and stuff?

Dragular   Ja . . . bats . . . unt stuff.

Harriet   Do it now.

Dragular   Vot?

Harriet   Do it now. Turn into a bat.

Dragular   Oh . . . um . . . nein. Is too . . . um . . . early.

(Silence. After a while they look at Eh?)

Crossbones   I guess he's a genie.

Harriet   There *was* a genie in our class. Can't remember his name though.   *(To Eh?)*   Hey, you! Hey?

(Eh? doesn't respond.)

Harriet   Hey, genie? *(She gets up and waves at him from right in front of his face)*   Hey, genie!   *(He looks up)*   What's your name?

Eh?   Eh?

Harriet   I said, what's your name?

Eh?   Eh?

Harriet   Your name! Your name!

Eh? My game? Badminton! I just love Badminton!

Harriet No! What are you called?

Eh? Of course I'm not bald! I wear this turban because I'm a genie.

Harriet No! No! *(She sighs)* Oh, forget it! Would you like a drink?

Eh? *(Offended)* Well, you'd stink too, if you spent most of your time shut up in an old bottle!

Harriet *(Frowning and sitting down)* I hope the others turn up soon!

Dragular Me too.

Harriet I don't know why I came actually. It's looking like a worse idea all the time.

Dragular Ven I got zat note from Herr Mandrake, ze head of ze school, I voz puzzled, for sure.

Harriet He said he was getting the old Monster Class of 1980 together, because he was feeling nostalgic. Seems odd. I always thought he hated us!

Crossbones I only came 'cause I was a bit tired of sittin' on seaweed, stranglin' people!

Harriet What do you think Professor Mandrake's got in mind?

Crossbones Beats me. Probably somethin' terribly gross-out.

Harriet You think so? I'm not really up to much tonight.

Crossbones We'll probably sit around talkin' about the old days! Remember? Learnin' all the skills we'd need when we went out into the world: stranglin', choppin' off heads, bitin' people in the neck, axe murders . . .

Harriet Yeah. I suppose so. I remember those days well. Good old Horror Hall Preparatory School For Terribly Nasty Monsters — the old alma mater, *eh*?

Eh? Sorry. Did you call me?

Harriet No. I was just talking about the school.

Eh? Don't call me a fool!

(Zee-Zee enters.)

Zee-Zee   Hey, is everyone here? Wow! Isn't this great? All together again. The old gang.

Dragular   Ah, Zee-Zee the Zombie.

Harriet   Hello, Zee-Zee. How's life? Oh, sorry, you're dead. I keep forgetting.

Zee-Zee   That's okay. Everyone forgets. I'm used to it.

Harriet   I was really glad to hear you'd passed on. You were majoring in Zombie, weren't you?

Zee-Zee   Sure was. Finally got there. I was run over by a bus, you know?

Crossbones   Yeah? How nice for ya? Talk about the easy way ta go! I 'ad to rot away at the bottom of the sea for ten years to get where I am today!

Zee-Zee   Oh, don't go on, Boney! You're still a grump, I see.

Crossbones   What of it?

(Enter Aloysius and Wendy.)

Wendy   Hi, everyone.

Zee-Zee   Wendy! Great to see you! You're looking really good. How's it goin'?

Wendy   Hello, Zee-Zee. It's going really . . . um . . . okay.

Harriet   You haven't changed much, Wendy. . .

Wendy   I know. That's the problem.

Harriet   You were taking the Werewolf course, weren't you? Is it a full moon tonight?

Wendy   No.   *(Aside)*   Thank goodness.

Crossbones   What a pity! Might've livened up the evenin'. Who's this weirdo you're with? Looks really out of it.

Wendy   Aloysius. You remember Aloysius? Two-headed alien from the planet Muckup?

Crossbones   Two-headed? He's only got one!

Aloysius   I did have two. But I got really excited one day last summer and lost my head. Haven't been able to find it since.

Crossbones   Really?   *(Points at Harriet)*   Maybe she could help you. She's a head-hunter. Ha! Ha!   *(No one laughs)*   It was a joke.

Harriet   It's been a good decade for monsters from outer space, hasn't it, Aloysius? First *Alien*, then *Aliens*, followed by *More Aliens*, and finally, *Heaps of Aliens* . . . plenty of blood and guts in those movies! Started a trend, *eh*?

Eh?   Did someone call me?

Harriet   No. I was talking to Aloysius.

Eh?   You bet I'm suspicious. You keep calling me!

Harriet   I do not!

Eh?   Don't call me a clot!

Wendy   *(To Harriet)*   Who *is* he?

Harriet   Eh? He's deaf. You were telling us about yourself, Aloysius? Terrorised any major cities lately?

Aloysius   Who me? Oh, yeah . . . sure. I . . . um . . . invaded . . . um . . . this township . . . um . . . just last week.

Crossbones   Was it in the papers?

Aloysius   Well, no. It wasn't a very big town. More of an isolated settlement.

Crossbones   Settlement?

Aloysius   A couple of kangaroos near Grubby Creek. I've been a bit ill. Losing my head really put me off terrorising.   *(He changes the subject by picking up a piece of paper from the table)*   According to this list, there's two more coming.

Harriet   Who?

Aloysius   Raven Maniac . . . and Donald Horror-Gruesome-Sicko Pus-Monster the Third!

(Suddenly we hear a clock — Big Ben type — tolling twelve.)

Crossbones   Look 'ere! It's just on midnight. Mandrake should've turned up by now.

Harriet   Yeah. I wonder when the party's going to start?

(A heavy door slams. Mandrake appears.)

Mandrake   Ha! Ha! Ha! At last, midnight has come. You're here, all of you — the hideous, pathetic, disgraceful class that's been a blot on my copybook ever since 1980.

Wendy   Professor Mandrake!

Eh?   *(Jumping up)*   Where's the snake?

Harriet   What do you mean 'disgraceful'?

Crossbones   Yeah. I thought we were called here to remember the good old days!

Mandrake   No! I've called you all here so that I'll never have to remember the good old days again!

Crossbones   Crikey, mate! What do ya mean?

Mandrake   I'm going to kill you all!

Zee-Zee   Oh, dear. That doesn't sound like much fun!

Mandrake   I should say not. You seven are the worst students I've ever had at this school — failures, all of you. You've been a living . . . and unliving . . . indictment of everything The Horror Hall Preparatory School For Terribly Nasty Monsters stands for — gore, horror, cruelty, misery. . . Your failure has made this school a laughing stock in the eyes of Horrible Society everywhere!

Aloysius   Failures? Hey, I resent that!

Crossbones   Yeah! I've been doing all right!

Dragular   Unt me!

Harriet   Wait! I think the Professor's right! I for one have got a confession to make. And I suspect we're all in the same boat!

Zee-Zee   A confession?

Harriet   Yes. I'm a failure as a rampaging horror. I've never cut off anybody's head. Sometimes I trim the roses, but that's as far as I'll go.

Mandrake   Very true, Harriet. Now, who else can deny that the same is true of themselves?

(Silence.)

Aloysius   Actually . . . now that you mention it . . . I'm a bit of a wash-out too. I mean, one-headed aliens who look like the guy next door are up against it to start with — but I really hate all that leaping out of people's chests and tearing them apart. Tried invading a nice little old lady's loungeroom once. She invited me to have tea and scones with her.

Zee-Zee   Well, now that you mention it . . . I'm not much chop as a zombie either. Frankly all that shuffling about bug-eyed with bits of me falling off doesn't turn me on at all. What a drag! Have you ever met one of those *Night of the Living Dead* bores! I want to have fun. Life's a real buzz . . . and so's death! I'm spooksperson for the Good Times Afterlife Society. Ever heard of it?

Mandrake   It's a perversity!

Zee-Zee   It's made up of lots of zombies who want to dance rather than shuffle, and ghosts who reckon all that haunting stuff is for the birds. They're high spirits all right — more into partying than shrieking and clanging chains.

Mandrake   See! None of you is successfully fantastic. Look at the genie . . . what's-'s-name. Deaf as a post.

Eh?   I'd love some toast. Starving, I am.

Mandrake   A deaf genie's worse than useless. One guy who rubbed Eh?'s bottle a while back asked for three wishes. He ended up with three old hags bent cackling over a cauldron! And another victim wanted to win the lottery. . . She found herself with a whole room full of clay bowls!

Crossbones   Yeah, well, I'm a failure too. I can't swim and I've got a terrible fear of water. Couldn't get anywhere near a sunken pirate ship. I work as a teaching aid in the anatomy section of the University.

Dragular   And me, I've never bitten anyone in my life. The sight of blood makes me squeamish. That's why they call me Dragular . . . I'm a real drag at blood-baths.

Harriet   What happened to your accent?

Dragular   It was a fake. I thought it'd make the vampire image a bit more convincing. I'm a teensy bit boring, you see. I collect stamps.

Crossbones   What about Wendy?

Wendy   I'm the same. I started training as a werewolf, because when I was young I turned into a one-way street during the full moon. I was hoping I could work my way up to something more impressive. The most I ever made it to was a slightly annoyed hamster.

Harriet   Wow! All of us, failures. Not a real horror amongst us.

Mandrake   Exactly! Of all your class only two of you are really worthy of being graduates of Horror Hall Preparatory School For Terribly Nasty Monsters . . .

Crossbones   Let me guess! Raven Maniac and Donald Horror-Gruesome-Sicko Pus-Monster the Third!

Mandrake   I've brought you all together so that those two, the only successful graduates of my school, can slaughter the rest of you, thus restoring my reputation. They're due any minute now, and when they see how wimpy you are they'll go mad with blood-lust and tear you limb from limb! My shame will be wiped out forever!

Wendy   I remember Raven. She was crazy. Used to chop up first year students and poison the canteen staff and pull other pranks like that. She trimmed her nails with an axe. She was studying to be a Mad Killer.

Harriet   What was Donald Horror-Gruesome-Sicko Pus-Monster the Third studying?

Aloysius   Grossness! He was planning to be so ugly that anyone looking at him would be instantly ill and die of terminal revulsion.

Wendy   He was well on the way too. What about his nose?

Aloysius   Which one?

Wendy   All of them!

Crossbones   Yuck! Last time I saw 'im 'is face was covered in warts.

Aloysius   That was when the course started. By his final year his whole head was a wart! He used to ooze people to death!

Harriet   We don't stand a chance!

(There is a heavy knocking on the door. It opens.)

Aloysius   Oh, no!

Wendy   Don't panic, Aloysius!

Mandrake   You'd better panic! This is them now — the most hideous and murderous pair ever to graduate from my school! At last the time for revenge has come!

(Raven Maniac and Donald Pus-Monster enter. They look really nice and not at all horrible.)

Mandrake   *(Not noticing)*   Ha! Ha! Ha! Kill them! Kill them all!

(The others scream and run about frantically.)

Raven   Hi! Great to see you all!

Donald   Yeah! Greetings everyone! You look nice!

Harriet   *(Stopping)*   Hang on! Stop panicking, you lot! I don't think it's as bad as we expected!

(The others stop and look at Raven and Donald in surprise.)

Harriet   *(To Raven and Donald)*   You've changed!

Mandrake   *(Stunned)*   Raven Maniac and Donald Horror-Gruesome-Sicko Pus-Monster the Third! What's happened to you? Aren't you going to kill them?

Others   Yeah. What's going on? Aren't you going to kill us?

Raven   Oh, sorry, but we couldn't possibly kill anyone!

Donald   Gosh, Professor, I hope we haven't spoilt your plans for the evening!

Mandrake   Why are you so nice? When you left my school back in 1980 you were the most horrible students I've ever had!

Raven   We saw the error of our ways. Our classmates were all so nice . . . and being rotten really made us feel bad.

Donald   When we saw how the others went out into the world and lived a good life, without even killing anyone, we thought we should give it a go too.

Raven   We made a real effort to improve ourselves and this is the result. Aren't you proud of us?

Mandrake   Oh, no! All my hopes . . . dashed!   *(He sobs)*

Harriet   *(Comforting him)*   Never mind, Professor. There's still one way you can turn your school into a success.

Mandrake   *(Hopefully)*   What's that?

Harriet   Change it from the Horror Hall Preparatory School For Terribly Nasty Monsters . . . to the Horror Hall Preparatory School For Really Nice People. Then you'll have a one hundred per cent success rate!

Mandrake   Oh, nooo!   *(Weeping)*

(Everyone cheers. Lights out.)

Questions

1 What does Crossbones say he spends his time doing?

2 How does Harriet say she spends her time?

3 What problem does Eh? have?

4 What are Mandrake's feelings about his class of 1980?

5 What does Mandrake plan to do to them?

6 Why does Harriet consider herself a failure?

7 Why does Crossbones think he is a failure?

8 Why is Dragular a failure?

9 Why was Donald Horror-Gruesome-Sicko Pus-Monster the Third so horrible to look at?

10 Why was Mandrake weeping at the end of the play?

11 Which character did you find most interesting? Why?

12 Do you think this play would be popular with students? Why?

ACKNOWLEDGEMENTS

The authors and publishers are grateful to the following for permission to reproduce copyright material:

Poetry and prose
Anvil Press Poetry Ltd for 'Number 14' from *Stations* by Keith Bosley (1979); Basil Blackwell for 'Space Pilot' by John Blackie; Betsy Byars and The Bodley Head for extracts from *The Eighteenth Emergency* and *The Pinballs* by Betsy Byars; Colin Thiele and Rigby Publishers for the extract from *Magpie Island*; Collins Dove for the extract from *As the Twig Is Bent* by Terry Lane; Constable Publishers for 'Releasing a Migrant Yen' translated by Arthur Waley in *170 Chinese Poems*; David Hamer for 'Alfie'; David Higham Associates Limited for 'Pegasus' by Eleanor Farjeon from *The Children's Bells*; Eurobooks Limited for the fables from *The Fables of Aesop* edited by Ruth Spriggs; Gerald Duckworth & Co Ltd for 'The Yak' from *Cautionary Verses* by Hilaire Belloc; Grafton Books for the extract from *A Zoo in My Luggage* by Gerald Durrell; Hamish Hamilton for the extract from *Freaky Friday* by Mary Rodgers; Ian Serraillier for 'The Challenge of the Green Knight'; James Kirkup for 'Thunder and Lightning'; Jonathan Cape Limited for 'Kipnapped' from *Light in the Attic* by Shel Silverstein; Kingfisher Books Limited for 'Hot Food' from the *Kingfisher Book of Children's Poetry* selected by Michael Rosen; Laura Cecil, Literary Agent for 'The Old Wife and the Ghost' from *James Reeves: The Complete Poems* and for the extract from *Heroes and Monsters* (Legends of Ancient Greece) by James Reeves; Lutterworth Press for the extract from *The Tale of Sir Gawain* by Neil Philip; Martin Secker & Warburg for 'One Gone, Eight to Go' by George Macbeth, from *Poems from Oby*; Methuen Children's Books for the extracts from *Journey of 1000 Miles* by Ian Strachen; Mike Gibson for 'The Mysterious Case of the Disappearing Wart'; Jean Kenward for 'Frog'; Sheila Simmons for 'Bread'; Wendy Cope for 'Kenneth'; Murray Pollinger for the extract from *Boy* by Roald Dahl; New Directions Publishing Corporation for 'The Mad Yak' by Gregory Corso from *Long Live Man*, copyright © 1962 by New Directions Publishing Corporation; Oxford University Press for 'The Late Express' by Barbara Giles, from *Upright Downfall: Poems by Barbara Giles*, Roy Fuller and Adrian Rumble (1983); Penguin Books (N.Z.) Limited for the extract from *The Silent One* by Joy Cowley; Penguin Books Australia Ltd for the extract from *Hating Alison Ashley: The Play* by Richard Tulloch and Robin Klein, the extract from *My Sister Sif* by Ruth Park, and for the extracts from *A Fortunate Life* by A. B. Facey; Penguin Books Limited for extracts from *Fables of Aesop* translated by S. A. Hanford (Penguin Classics, 1954), copyright © S. A. Handford, 1954; Penguin Books Ltd for the extract from *Frozen Fire* by James Houston; Rhyll McMaster for 'Underneath the House'; Robert Morgan and Campbell Thomson & McLaughlin Limited for 'Uncle

Bert' by Robert Morgan; Shelagh McGee for 'Wanted — A Witch's Cat' from *What Witches Do* by Shelagh McGee; Spike Milligan Productions Ltd for 'If I Die in War' by Spike Milligan; The Currency Press for the extracts from *A Fortunate Life — The Play* by Clem Gorman; Vernon Scanell for 'The Long Flight'; W. N. Scott for 'The Old Man's Song' and 'Frogs'; William Heinemann Ltd for the extract from *To Kill a Mockingbird* by Harper Lee.

Advertisements, photographs, book covers and cartoons
Alan Foley Pty Ltd for the cartoons on pp. 26, 129, 140, 158 bottom; Andrew Chapman for the photographs on pp. 90, 91 bottom left and right, 118, 126, 240; Associated Press and The West Australian for the photograph and article on p. 145; Collins Educational for the cover on p. 220; David Moore for the photograph on p. 193; Dove Communications Pty Ltd for the cover on p. 75; Gaffney International Licensing Pty Ltd for the cartoons on pp. 156, 158 top, 210; Heinemann Educational Ltd for the cover on p. 5; Lutterworth Press for the cover on p. 9; Macmillan Accounts and Administration Ltd for the covers on pp. 46, 162, 168, 227; News Limited for the photograph on p. 105; North America Syndicate Inc. for the cartoon on p. 157; Océ Australia Ltd for the advertisement on p. 155; Pan Books for the cover on p. 2; PBL Marketing for the photographs on pp. 71, 96 from *The Making of A Fortunate Life*; Puffin Books for the covers on pp. 40, 42, 72, 78, 106, 109, 113, 165, 194, 197, 199, 224; Stock Photos for the photograph on pp. 38–39; The Herald and Weekly Times Ltd for the photographs on p. 91 top, 160–1; The West Australian for the photograph and article on pp. 142.

While every care has been taken to trace and acknowledge copyright, the publishers tender their apologies for any accidental infringement where copyright has proved untraceable. They would be pleased to come to a suitable arrangement with the rightful owner in each case.

Illustrations by Carol Pelham-Thorman and Rick Amor

Cover design and photograph by Jan Schmoeger